List It Like A Pro

How to Sell Your House for More Money in Less Than 30 Day

FREE BONUS

As an appreciation for getting a copy of my book, I'd like to offer you a Complete Listing Consultation, including a FSBO Signage Kit, and Free Consultation to price your home, develop a marketing campaign, and help you find buyers!
ALL FREE – No Gimmicks, Tricks, or Strings Attached.

I will literally walk you through every step of this book to get you started on the path to selling your home quick and profitably.

To get your free kit, or learn more, visit

The SWFL Relocation Team

Author's Preface

I bought my first house for $155,000. Two years later I fired my agent, found another, and sold it for $189,000, $5,000 above asking price, in a buyer's market. I put less than $10,000 of materials into the house.

How did I do it?

I grew up in a small little farming town in Connecticut called East Windsor. It was so small that most people in Connecticut had never heard of it. But it was home to me and I wouldn't have traded growing up there for anything.

One of the greatest lessons I learned from that town is that hard work does pay off, and it's a lesson I've carried with me all my life.

It's how we upset one of the best teams in the state and won our schools first state championship in nearly 30 years.

It's how I learned to build 12 custom homes every summer with a crew of 4. It's how I've been able to literally make every one of my clients a raving fan.

And it's how I stripped and finished all the wood floors, painted all the rooms, remodeled the entire kitchen and bathroom, revived the lawn and landscaping, fixed all the doors, and replaced the furnace, for less than $10,000.

But making that profit wasn't just hard work.

See when I built those houses every summer and winter break throughout high school, I was taken under the wing of one of the best custom home-builder's in the state. He taught me how to read blueprints, build a house from the ground up, and develop a keen eye for design and craftmanship.

After high school I worked for a home remodeling company during my semester breaks from college and learned the finer side of home building and all the intricacies and details that go into finishing a home. And in my free time I'd study books written by some of the greatest minds in the real estate investment industry, slowly gathering more and more knowledge.

Then I started my own remodeling company as a general contractor in Connecticut and remodeled homes on my own, so I learned how to estimate materials and labor costs, and could then figure out what a home was actually worth on the market.

So when it finally came time for me and my fiancé to buy a home, I had a wealth of knowledge about what I was looking for in a home, how much I was willing to pay, and how much work I was willing to do on the home.

What I didn't know was anything about the home-buying process. So, we did what most people do...called up the friend of the family, and asked for his help. And while we had a tight budget, it was surprising at how quickly he was able to find something for us.

It ended up being a pocket-listing so he would be negotiating both sides. I obviously felt torn about this because he was trying to negotiate a common ground for both of us, but in the end I felt like we ended up getting the better end of the stick.

Two years later when we went to sell, we found his pricing suggestion to be extremely low for the improvements we had made. We shopped around and in less than a week after signing with another agent, the home sold for $5,000 above what we were asking.

Keep in mind, while I only spent around $10,000 in materials, I worked on the home for 2 years and brought a ton of experience with me to each improvement I made.

And that's what I offer my clients.

I'm not just bringing the my license and understanding of Real Estate law and contracts. While those are extremely important and something I focus heavily on in the beginning to keep my clients safe, it's only a portion of the job.

I bring over a decade of residential construction and home-improvement experience. I bring a wealth of experience in digital marketing, social media marketing, and local outreach.

I've built a sizable network of buyer and seller agents throughout the country, as well as real estate services and vendors to help answer your questions and provide you high-quality service for all your needs.

And most important of all, I bring my work ethic. There isn't an agent around who will outwork me, and I guarantee you peace of mind throughout our journey together in this book and beyond.

Introduction – Why Didn't My House Sell?

Seller A and Seller B are both best friends with very similar homes on a quiet middle-class cul-de-sac in Anytown, USA. Both bought their homes in a buyer's market and paid $245,000 for their homes nearly 5 years ago, though they hadn't done much to improve the home since.

They both had the dream of moving up north to a cabin in the woods where they can enjoy fishing, hunting, and cold beers by a lake.

After a few weeks of thinking it over, Seller A decided if he was ever going to make the move, it had to be now, or he would never do it.

Seller A searched on Google for a nearby real estate agent, and within a week, the house was listed on the market for $287,000.

Seller B decided he was going to wait and see how Seller A's house and agent did in the market.

After 2 months, Seller A dropped the price of his home again, this time from $280,000 to $270,000, making it a total decrease of $17,000 since listing it.

With no buyers even considering making an offer, and only a couple weeks left on the listing agreement, Seller A was anxious, irritated, and sick of his agent.

It seemed like all he kept hearing was that he had to drop the price.

Right down the street, Seller B had been watching Seller A's price keep dropping and listening to his friends complaints about his agent.

After listening to his complaints and the things he felt like the agent should be doing or at least have done differently, Seller B decided he was going to take that information and try selling his home on his own.

He listed his house as a **For Sale By Owner** (FSBO) at $275,000.

Within 2 days, Seller B had an offer for $265,000, but decided to reject the offer and wait for a better one since the house had only been on the market for 2 days.

After 2 months, he finally got another offer for $260,000 and was able to counter and negotiate it up to $263,000.

Seller A stayed on the market and accepted an offer around the time Seller B accepted his. Seller A settled for $263,000.

The Typical Seller Dilemmas

Seller A and Seller B demonstrate the two most common types of seller's whose homes don't sell.

A lot happened in those two stories, so let's break them down to see what happened and what common mistakes these two sellers made.

The Common Elements

Both sellers had similar homes, in the same neighborhood, with the same home value that they both purchased around the same time, 5 years earlier.

Neither had made any improvements to the house, but they did buy them in a seller's market, which indicates that their home value likely increased since. How much it increased is still unclear.

Seller A

Seller A hired an agent, but listed it at $287,000, a $42,000 price increase.

While this price increase could very well happen with some major improvements, inflation, and a shift to a seller's market, the likelihood of the price increasing that much in just 5 years without any improvements is low.

If that is the case, we know that either the listing agent lost the listing price battle to the homeowner, or the listing agent didn't know his or her market. **In either case, he hired the wrong agent.**

In most cases, *homeowners tend to overvalue their property because of the emotional connection to it*, and a newer agent, or agent who really wants the listing, will agree to the homeowners listing price.

Overpricing a home can be detrimental to it selling quickly and profitably, but we will discuss this later in the book.

Seller B

Seller B decided to wait 2 months before going to market, and when he did, he chose to list it himself in order to save the headaches and commission.

Seller B listed the home for $10,000 less than Seller B, which was a good move because of how little action he saw Seller A's home getting at the higher price point.

The mistake in this story is not taking, or at least countering, the first offer.

While it wasn't quite the price he was looking for, **most buyers leave themselves some room to negotiate.**

In addition, the **statistics show that often the first offer is the best offer.**

By declining the offer and waiting for a better offer, Seller B lost 2 more months of mortgage payments, utilities, taxes, and insurance premiums on top of having to accept an offer lower than the first one after negotiations.

That extra 2 months easily cost the Seller $3000 in bills and at the very least an additional $2000 in the initial offer. If Seller B countered the first offer, he very well may have negotiated the price up to $268,000.

In both stories, the sellers walked away with a profit for having put almost no money back into the house, but they both left money on the table and waited longer than they would have liked to sell their homes.

That is why I wrote this book.

When both sellers were unable to sell their homes, which is more often the case than these story outcomes, I am the one usually stepping in to clean up the mess.

My three main questions to these sellers would have been:

1. **What was the price and how did you arrive at it?**

2. **What was your pricing strategy?**

3. **What was the marketing strategy?**

Right off the bat I would have known exactly why the houses weren't selling.

When asked what the original listing price was and how they arrived at it, both would have confessed that they had set the price and based it on what they felt it was worth and the time they had owned it. Seller B would have adjusted the price based on Seller A's activity.

That's strike one.

As for the pricing strategy, they both wanted to price it a little on the high side to start out and drop over time if they needed hoping that someone would make an offer early on for what they were ideally willing to sell it for.

That's strike two.

And as it is with most homeowners, Seller A really didn't know much about what the agent was doing for the marketing.

He knew that the agent had hosted an open house, and had the home listed in the MLS and other big search sites but wasn't sure of the methods and strategies the agent was using.

He confessed that he had found this agent nearby on Google and hired him without shopping around.

That was strike three.

They were out of ideas and out of time.

What I do on a surface level is help homeowners sell their homes for maximum profit in minimal time.

But what I do on a deep level is build relationships with people and help them meet their goals. While profit and time are both important factors in real estate, even more important are the reasons behind selling a home.

For some it means leaving behind the decades of memories they've shared with family and friends, and there's no price they could ever put on that.

For some it means relocating to another state to start a new job, or a family near loved ones.

For others, it might mean starting a new chapter in their life without the person they've built a life around.

Those kinds of reasons for selling aren't just about numbers. It's about a story, emotion, meaning, uncertainty. Those are vulnerable times in people's lives, and it's my job to make those transitions smooth and stress-free.

And while I can't personally help every homeowner work through those transitions and ensure a smooth selling experience, I *CAN* teach them how to do it on their own—I can teach them what they should be looking for and what they should be expecting from a great real estate agent.

This book will give you the exact process I use to prepare, market, and sell our clients' homes in less than 30 days.

What You Will Learn:

- How to prepare your home for listing including cleaning and staging tips and resources

- How to eliminate late-process snags and deal-breakers

- What paperwork you will need to list your house or condo

- How to price your home strategically to sell quickly, for high profit

- How to list and market your home to the largest number of ideal buyers

- How to create attractive ads and marketing materials for little or no money

- How to field offers, respond, and negotiate effectively

- How to navigate the transaction, paperwork, and deadlines for a smooth closing

- And much more

After watching not only my own clients, but buyers and sellers throughout the industry, lose deal after deal over issues that could have been taken care of before the home was ever listed, I began working with my partner Dave Bernard on a unique approach to selling homes—a process that would eliminate the 3 major reasons deals fall through.

Those reasons are:

- ✓ **The bank didn't approve the home for financing**

- ✓ **The home didn't appraise**

- ✓ **The inspection revealed issues that either the buyer or seller wasn't willing to negotiate on**

We just needed a process that fixed these issues up front instead of at the end. And that's how we created our Pre-Assurance Program—the very program I'm going to teach you how to use throughout this book.

How This Book Is Setup

This book is short because it's a no-nonsense approach to selling your home. I don't like my time to be wasted, and when it comes to selling your home, neither should you. Time costs money.

For that very reason, I've only included the necessary steps to selling your home quickly and profitably. I have only included pictures of marketing materials when I felt they were absolutely necessary to your understanding.

Throughout the book, I will show you how to sell your home on your own, if that is your goal, but I will also show you what to look for in an agent if you plan on working with one.

There are many advantages to using an agent, and throughout this book you will see boxes labeled **REALTOR Advantage,** like the one below, that will explain some of the benefits working with a listing agent can provide you.

REALTOR Advantage Box

These excerpts will touch on advantages, tools, and insights agents have that are not available to unlicensed individuals. These advantages can speed up the selling process, reduce liability, improve your profit margin, and make the selling experience smooth and stress free.

In the back of the book I have also included appendices of supplemental materials and samples that will help you understand material in the book, or help you in the selling process.

Throughout the book I make several references to the appendices and encourage you to complete any worksheets as you read through the book. These worksheets will be crucial in completing steps later in the book.

What To Expect From This Book

Selling a home isn't free and it isn't easy—if it were, there wouldn't be more than 1.3 million real estate agents in the U.S. alone.

With that in mind, I'm a professional REALTOR. That means I take my job, my ethics, and the quality of work I do, very seriously, and while I can show you **exactly how to sell your home in less than 30 days**, it will require you to invest a little time, money, and effort up front.

While it may be tempting to skip steps or cut corners, I strongly encourage you stick to the blueprint as closely as possible. Be honest with yourself when building your price and pricing strategy—the market never lies.

If you need help with any of the steps in this book, feel free to send me an email with your questions at **Rick@SWFLRelocationTeam.com**, and either myself, or one of my team members will be happy to assist you.

Above all, whether you are working with an agent or on you own, this book is going to ask you to be an integral and invested part of the selling process.

There's nothing worse than an agent and homeowner not being on the same page with a listing, or worse, at odds. Many opportunities can fall through the cracks in either case.

What it cannot and will not do is teach you how to fill out contracts, renovate and flip a home, or list it as a rental property.

This book is strictly for homeowners selling a property, whether it's a primary, secondary, or investment property.

While I may be able to provide advice or suggestions for some of these other topics, they fall outside the scope of this book, and honestly, my scope of practice.

Making your home a no-brainer, for any buyer, is therefore the first step to List It Like A Pro!

Chapter 1 – Working with An Agent

While this book has been written with the intention of helping homeowners sell their home on their own, not everyone is going to want to put in the time, money, and effort into marketing and selling their own home.

If you plan on selling your own home, you can skip this first chapter. If you feel later on, after reading through the steps that you'd rather hire a listing agent, feel free to come back to this chapter to discover what you should be looking for in an agent, how to interview them, and what they should be doing for you on a consistent basis.

The Advantages of Working with An Agent

One of the most appealing advantages of working with a real estate agent is being able to worry less. While working with an agent may seem stressful at times, when compared to selling a house on your own, there's no comparison.

You don't have to create your own marketing materials and plan, schedule showings and coordinate with other agents or buyers, handle the transaction paperwork, handle negotiations, and many other time-consuming tasks that detract from your own life.

Agents also provide you with an additional layer of protection against lawsuits because they are much more familiar with real estate law and contracts. While mistakes do happen regarding real estate law, unlicensed homeowners tend to get themselves in trouble with real estate law much more frequently and make some very costly mistakes unintentionally.

Simple mistakes can cost inexperienced homeowners tens, if not hundreds, of thousands of dollars in damages or losses, and the liability is 100% on them.

Agents make the buying and selling process much faster, simpler, and stress-free for homeowners. While this may come at a cost (a commission), often, that cost is much less than less the average For Sale by Owner (FSBO) sells for versus a Realtor's sale price for the same property.

The National Association of Realtors (NAR) has some statistics on For Sale By Owner homes versus Realtor-assisted sales that are worth checking out.

What You'll Give Up When Working with An Agent

The biggest reason most people want to try selling their home on their own is because real estate agents work for a commission—generally around 6%, split between the buying and selling agent.

That commission can add up to a decent amount depending on the price of the home, and some homeowners would rather not pay that if they don't have to, which is understandable.

Other than that though, the only other drawback of using an agent is that you will lose some of the control over the transaction, marketing, and scheduling of the process.

It's not always easy working with people and this can become stressful and maddening if you don't hire the right person for the job.

In the end, it's ultimately up to you to decide whether the financial commitment is worth the liability and toll it will take on your personal life.

Searching for An Agent

With so much free information on the internet today, and so many people giving feedback and reviews, a search engine is a great place to start your search. Simply type in "real estate agents near me," and you'll find a list of agents that will pop up on the map.

Look through the list for agents that have 4 and 5-star reviews.

Don't just look at the rating though, see how many reviews they have received, and read through them to see if they have any substantial commentary on the agent.

Make a list of your top 5-6 agents from Google, or whichever search engine you use, because you are going to begin filtering them out.

Next, you're going to stalk them on social media. Yes, I said stalk. Friend request them if you have to, but you want access to see what they do on social media, who they are, and what they value.

Look them up on major social media sites that you have access to. It may even be worth creating an account just for research purposes on the platforms you don't have access to—Facebook, Instagram, Twitter, LinkedIn, YouTube, and Snapchat.

Another great place to look them up is Amazon. See if they have published any books.

Check out podcast platforms like Apple Podcasts, Stitcher, Google Podcasts, and Spotify.

All these platforms are marketing avenues and potential audiences that an agent can connect with and broadcast your home to.

They don't need to have massive audiences to reach many people. They only need to have a dedicated pool of audience members who know, like, and trust them.

This core group of people is essentially an army at their disposal to market your home, because that audience will help them with likes, comments, shares, and reviews that will catch others attention.

It's compound marketing.

Each of these platforms provides you with a point of reference to do a superficial background check. You want to see if they:

- Present themselves the way you would want your agent to represent your property,

- Are active in the community and on social media,

- Have a strong work ethic in their professional life,

- Or have a personal life that could detract from their ability to sell your home.

I also encourage you to look up their license on the state website to ensure that it is valid and see if they have, or have had, any lawsuits filed against them in the past.

A quick Google search of their names is also a good idea to see if any related articles or news stories pop up.

Weigh the pros and cons of each agent and narrow it down to your top 2-3 agents.

I always encourage clients to shop around and meet with multiple agents.

While an agent may look good on paper, you want to get to know them a little and make sure that you like them, and ultimately trust them.

Conducting Listing Appointment Interviews

Most listing agents have a process and presentation they like to go through with their prospective clients. They have questions, just as you have questions, and they want to make sure you are as good a fit for them as they are for you.

The sad reality is agents sometimes should fire themselves because they aren't a good fit for their client's needs.

While the agent is conducting the walkthrough evaluation and running through their own sets of questions, there are questions that you need to have answered as well, and the questions below should be at the core of your interview whether on the phone or in-person.

1. **What has your experience been in real estate and selling homes?**

   This question will break the ice and is open-ended so the agent can expand on their experience more.

2. **What area or home type do you specialize in?**

   A good agent should specialize in a niche and area. One who says they sell everywhere generally is the jack of all trades and the master of none.

3. **What sets you apart from other agents in this area and your brokerage?**

   This question might throw them off a bit, but they should have at least 2 or 3 things setting them apart that sound unique.

4. **What is the market like right now?**

   Any agent that says it's good, or it's tough, doesn't really know. How good the market is, depends on a host of variables (type of home, the location, size, etc.). A good agent will tell you that it depends and will ask follow-up questions give you a more precise answer.

5. **What are some unique marketing strategies you've used in the past?**

   There should be at least 1 marketing strategy mentioned that you haven't thought of. If you've thought of them all, then they aren't that unique considering this is their job.

6. **How comfortable are you with writing complex contracts?**

    Contracts can get tricky and they are the main line of defense should any legal issues arise during the selling process. You are going to want an agent who is very familiar with contracts and negotiating them.

7. **Do you work as an agent full-time?**

    Your best bet is having an agent who is full time because those agents are fully invested in the sale of your home—it's their livelihood on the line.

8. **What other partners would you work with to sell my home?**

    Good agents partner with professional photographers, appraisers, contractors, inspectors, title companies, and mortgage companies to sell your home. Make sure they have a good network that can not only help you but help your buyers if the need arises.

9. **How many clients are you currently representing?**

    It's good for an agent to have clients, but too many will hinder the attention they can give to marketing your home.

10. **Another agent said they could sell my home for $75K more at a smaller commission. Could you do that too?**

This question is asking them to not only defend their convictions and stand by their own value but see if they really know the market. A good agent knows their worth and knows a home value should be within a realistic range.

If you feel like the interview went well, make note of it, but don't settle for the first agent or the first interview that went well.

Follow-through and meet with all the agents you scheduled, and then decide.

Selling your home is a big and important decision and choosing the wrong agent can cost you big time.

And if you have decided to work with an agent, the rest of this book should be a reference point as to what a great agent should be doing for you.

For you brave men and women doing it on your own, we need to first make your home the hottest listing on the market.

Chapter 2 – Make Your Home A No-Brainer

When I was just 26, I made $30,000 on my first home. It wasn't a crazy amount of money, but it was a big profit considering how long I owned the home and how much money I put back into it.

It sat on about a third of an acre lot with a decent-sized backyard, had a white picket fence, and shutters on all the windows. While it was just over 1,100 square feet of living space, it had a finished basement of equal size.

When my fiancé and I first saw the home, despite its sun-scorched yard, and weathered curb-appeal, we knew when we walked in that this was the place.

We had been looking for about 6 months at different homes on the market but were looking for something specific.

We wanted a quaint starter home in a quiet, kid-friendly neighborhood, with at least 2 bedrooms and a den, 1 and a half bathrooms, tile or wood floors, and storage space.

The floors had some cracked tiles and severely worn wood from the previous owners' dogs running through the house. The bathroom needed to be updated and the wall colors, a neon orange, needed to be repainted.

Despite the amount of time and effort I knew this home was going to require, I recognized, from my experience as a general contractor, that it wouldn't take much money to accomplish.

The largest expense was going to be a new oil burner we would need to purchase within the next year.

We could see that it was priced to sell at just $155,900, and I knew that being in a volatile home market, we could easily turn a large profit when the market shifted.

Within two years we added $10,000 in improvements, including a complete bathroom remodel, refinishing the floors, repainting the whole house, landscaping, and rejuvenating the yard, and refacing the kitchen cabinets and hardware. We turned around and sold it for $185,000, with multiple bids and the winning bid coming in $5,000 over asking price and paying all closing costs.

How did we do it?

More importantly, how can you do it with your own home?

Planning the Journey

As it is with investing in the stock market, you want to buy low and sell high. And the only way you will know if it's a good time to buy or sell a home is if you've been watching the market and have done your homework on the homes, you're interested in.

If you have an agent, you can simply ask them what kind of market you are currently in.

If you don't have an agent, you could still call one and ask, but you can also look online. Search for "housing market analysis in (your area)."

Another way is to look at the inventory of homes. *If you can see that there are a larger number of homes under contract or being sold every week than there are homes being listed for sale, you know you are in a* **seller's market**. The demand is higher for homes than are currently available.

The opposite is true for a **buyer's market**.

It doesn't matter if you paid $500,000 for your home last year, if the market just crashed like it did in 2008, and you want to, or need to, sell right now, it might only be worth $250,000.

As I briefly mentioned earlier, we, as homeowners, tend to feel that our home is worth much more than it may be. Whether or not that is the case, **the market is really what dictates the home's "Fair Market Value."**

Fair-market value states that a buyer isn't going to pay anymore for a house than they must. If they can find the same house in an area nearby at a lower price, they are going to choose that other house over yours, every time.

And once that home is gone, other buyers and agents are going to compare the sale price to your home's asking price, deem it overpriced, and continue searching elsewhere.

But, while price may be one of the most important factors to get perfect, it's not where we need to start.

The first thing you need to understand is where your home stands, and what its strengths and weaknesses are, compared to other homes in your neighborhood and your town.

You'll need to examine both strengths and weaknesses, because you need to be able to understand who the home would be ideal for, and who it would not be ideal for. If you don't know who it is, and is not ideal for, you and your agent, will be wasting precious time, effort, and possibly money, marketing it to people who won't, and may not ever be interested in it. You need to really narrow down and understand who your perfect buyer is.

Start with The End in Mind

Starting with the end in mind means determining your ideal profit margin, ideal buyer, timeline, and deducing a maximum budget.

Timeline is a very important factor in determining the price of listing your home and your budget.

Whether you pay for repairs or not, there will be expenses in selling your home, some not so obvious, but expenses nonetheless—the mortgage and utilities for example, taxes, HOA or condo fees while the home sits on the market, the commission, any repairs that need to be done to pass code, or financing and appraisal.

Most homeowners forget about these costs, but they can reduce a home's profit rather quickly spread out over a couple of months sitting on the market—especially if you're not living there or you don't have anyone renting the unit.

In other situations, buyers may pay full price but ask you to cover certain expenses up front.

Bottom line, selling a home takes money, one way or the other, so I recommend coming to terms with it now and putting together a budget.

Appendix I in the back of the book has a short budget worksheet that will walk you through developing a budget to sell your home. Complete as much of this sheet as possible now before moving on.

Next part you need to look at who this home would be ideal for.

Defining Your Target Market

Using my first home as the example, it was only an 1100 square foot home, so this wasn't going to be a great home for a large family or a family with more than 2 teenage children—there just wasn't enough room.

It wasn't a luxury home located in an up and coming neighborhood with tons of amenities, so it wasn't going to be the best choice for affluent or retired couples who are looking for a socially active community.

What it did have was three beds and one and a half baths, plenty for a small family, newly married couple, or couple who were looking to start a family. It had a nice backyard that was fenced in with a white picket fence. It was in a very quiet neighborhood that was in the suburbs but was close to the city.

To help you work through your ideal marketing audience, I've created an **Avatar Profile Worksheet**, which can be found in Appendix II at the back of the book.

It will walk you through how to build an avatar profile which will help you better understand who your home is ideal for and how to build your marketing campaigns around. If you are working with an agent, they should be doing this for you and going over it with you.

This step is important because as you start marketing your home, especially when it comes to social media and paid ads, you're going to want to target specific groups of people so that you're not wasting your money and your agent isn't wasting his or her money.

It will also allow you to reach the widest audience of people who would be interested in this home and reduce the time and effort used chasing tire-kickers and leads that won't respond.

Plus, with so many different social media platforms nowadays, there's tons of ways for you as a homeowner to help your agent market and promote your own home.

You can join Facebook groups, add hashtags to your Facebook, Instagram, or Twitter posts, add it to Pinterest boards and much more.

Knowing your target audience allows you to focus in on what groups, what boards, hashtags, or platforms to target.

Invest Now and Earn More Later

The next step to prepare your home and make it a no-brainer, is to be proactive about getting it to market in the best possible condition. This is where you'll want to make an investment in your home and your listing it sells very quickly, with little to no stress or haggling.

I don't mean investing thousands of dollars into remodeling your kitchen and baths, replacing your AC, or other types of HGTV projects.

The investments I highly recommend to my selling clients cost less than $700 total—a home inspection, a home appraisal, and a title search, as well as the option of having required repairs made which we call "pre-hab."

My partner, Dave, and I call this our **"Pre-Assurance Package,"** and I'll be referring to it throughout the book.

We credit our seller's back at closing for their up-front investments because we know they are going to pay dividends in the end and practically guarantee the closing.

This might be something you can negotiate with your own listing agent as well, so don't be afraid to ask.

While these are typically done on the back-end of a deal and are usually up to the buyer and their lender to have completed, as we discussed earlier in the book, these are also the most common reasons the deal fall apart.

You can list it without these investments and hope the deal doesn't fall apart, or you can spend the $700 up front, close the deal on time, and save another month of utility bills, taxes, mortgage payments, and other expenses.

Getting these things done up-front makes your home so much more attractive and marketable.

Put yourself in a buyer's shoes. You're searching for a home and you've found several on Zillow. One of the properties has a description that says inspection, appraisal, and title search already completed and the documents will be provided on request.

Would you feel more comfortable with making an offer on that home if you know that it has already gone through an inspection and has had repairs made? Of course, you would.

REALTOR Story - A Flipping Nightmare

Two of my clients told me about a horrible experience they had purchasing an investment property.

It was a short-sale and against their better judgement, skipped the home inspection, believing the profit margin was plenty to cover the renovations they would need after their walkthrough and calculations.

As soon as they had closed the deal and owned the home, the town slapped the home with several major code violations which ended up eliminating their projected profit margin almost entirely.

While they had figured in the renovations for the flip, these violations cost them thousands and thousands of dollars they never recouped. They essentially sold the home at cost and wasted a lot of money that could have earned interest somewhere else, and time they'll never get back.

Whether the home inspection would have saved them from making the purchase in the first place is a moot point, but it may have given them some things to consider prior to purchasing or at the very least some information about past renovations that may have given them cause to do a little more digging.

At the very least they broke even and could chalk it up to experience, but there are tons of stories where the losses are devastating.

With these small investments, you don't need to worry about if permits have been pulled for all the projects, if the home will pass FHA/VA inspections, or it will appraise for the offer price.

A buyer may want to have their own inspection done and their lender may require their own appraisal, but you won't have to worry about the deal falling through for one of these common reasons.

In addition, it also eliminates a buyer's use of contingencies when you know they won't be able to exercise them. So, it streamlines and practically guarantees the sale and closing on any offer that is accepted.

I've included a quick-reference Home Inspection Guide in Appendix V so you know how to find a great inspector and exactly what they should be checking for, especially in Southwest Florida.

So, while these investments may cost you a couple hundred dollars up front, they will also save you a lot of time and effort in the end when it comes time to close.

Think about how much money a quick sale is saving you too. If you already forgot, look back at the budget worksheet under carry costs.

Once you've had these inspections done, you're in a better position to analyze your home's position in the market and decide whether there are projects that need to be completed to make your home universally sellable, or room for value-increasing projects to maximize your profit.

Afterall, isn't that the idea of selling to hopefully earn a high ROI?

Chapter 3 – Maximizing Your Return on Investment (ROI)

I'm going to tell you a quick little story and I want you to tell me what's wrong with it.

Seller A was thinking about putting her house on the market and wanted to get an opinion on what it could sell for "As-Is."

Her long-time friend and real estate agent, Agent Smith, stopped by to do a walkthrough and comparative market analysis. He told her he thought it was worth somewhere around $250,000.

Disappointed, she asked how he was justifying that figure.

Agent Smith told her that while other homes that had a similar footprint, number of beds and baths, and features were selling for around $280,000 in her neighborhood, her kitchen was outdated and small, the floors were carpet throughout, which most people didn't want anymore, the windows and doors were original and needed to be replaced, and the home was 20 years older than many of the others on the market.

After a few days of brewing over the feedback, Seller A decided that out of all of the features in her home, the kitchen would make the biggest impact on the home since it was the central point of the home, and offered the simplest way to close the value gap.

She figured if she could upgrade her kitchen to a $30,000 kitchen and replace the carpeted flooring with a vinyl floating floor, she could close the gap and get what she really wanted for the house.

I've said enough.

What's wrong with this story?

How about the fact that it doesn't make sense to pay for a $30,000 kitchen and replace the flooring.

While this may seem like a silly story, you wouldn't believe how many people have made mistakes like this or worse.

They watch an HGTV episode and decide the kitchen or bathroom could be upgraded and that is what's going to help them get the price they'd like to sell for. That couldn't be farther from the truth.

Profit Takes Priority

Nobody buys a house to throw away money, so naturally maximizing our profit and return on investment is most likely one of the top priorities when selling a home, but there's nothing worse than investing in home improvement projects to find out you'll never recoup that money.

While there are many good reasons for updating your home and investing in home improvement projects, doing them because that's what everyone does on HGTV's Los Angeles house flipping show is not one of them.

The first thing to realize is that there is no home improvement project that will provide you with a 100% return on investment—at least not in real value. That means you aren't likely to recoup the money you spend on the true value of their home.

However, there are some projects that can return their investment in perceived value to a buyer, and those are the types of investments that pay off.

Things like updating a bathroom or upgrading a kitchen can provide a lot of perceived value to a buyer, however, completely remodeling a kitchen or bath is in many cases not going to be worth the investment.

Not to worry though. A little later in this chapter I've provided some simple and cost-effective ideas for giving your home a facelift and investing in projects that will multiply your return on investment.

What Projects Are Worth It?

Every project is different and will have different rates of return on investment, but most projects aren't worth the cost when compared to their improvement value.

I've listed the top 5 home improvement projects that have the highest return on investment below to give you an idea of what I mean.

According to the Remodeling 2020 Cost vs. Value Report the top 5 projects are in Southwest Florida:

1. Roofing Replacement – Average Recoup - 80%

2. Siding Replacement – Average Recoup - 77.6%

3. Window Replacement – Average Recoup - 76.7%

4. Deck Addition – Average Recoup - 76.6%

5. Minor Kitchen Remodel – Average Recoup - 66.9%

As you can see, these projects don't always provide you with the recoupment you expect.

So, that $20,000 midrange kitchen remodel is only going to provide your house with an extra $13,000 in value.

Not so enticing when you look at it that way, huh?

If you have questions on projects you've been thinking about doing in your home, I highly recommend checking out the Cost vs. Value Reports prior.

You can check the average cost, resale value, and recoup of most major projects and search by specific cities and regions throughout the US.

Which Projects Should I Do?

If you've followed this blueprint and invested in getting the inspection, appraisal and title search done, as suggested in Chapter 2, you'll have a much better idea of where to start and what steps to take next to reach the widest audience of buyers.

Once you get your inspection report, you'll want to discuss the report with both the inspector and your listing agent, if you have one.

I recommend dividing any issues on the report into 3 categories: **Required, Suggested, and ROI projects.**

Required Projects

Required projects are the projects you need to complete to meet the requirement of buyers and their financing programs.

There are several different financing options for buyers and the requirements a home must meet varies in each program. **FHA and VA financing packages tend to be the strictest**, requiring homes to meet higher standards with inspection and appraisal.

Something as small and simple as chipping or peeling paint can be the only reason a home doesn't get approved for these kinds of programs, so in order to reach the widest audience, you'll need to know everything that needs to be done to pass such financing program standards.

In certain states, the **VA Loan program may also require the seller to pay certain fees** the veteran is not allowed to pay.

You may want to check with your local lenders to see if these fees will apply before you list your home so you already know if you will be willing to entertain a VA financing offer.

Required projects don't include things like buying brand new appliances just because the current set is old or outdated. If it is in working condition at the time of inspection, the buyers really don't have any leverage or an out if you use the right contract.

That doesn't mean they can't or won't ask you for repairs, replacements, or credits at closing—because many will—but it does mean that you are not obligated to do so. Whether you agree to their terms or not, the buyers will still be required to fulfill the contract or lose their deposit.

For this very reason, I suggest making sure you have a great agent or lawyer who knows real estate contracts inside and out.

It's also why **I suggest requiring a minimum of 3-5% earnest money deposit**—so the buyer has some skin in the game, and you know they are serious about buying your home.

Suggested Projects

Suggested projects and repairs are generally things you should do to not only make your home more marketable, but to make it safer, more functional, or bring it up to date.

This could be something as simple as patching holes in the drywall or replacing lightbulbs and fixtures, or even replacing door handles, cabinet hardware, and the like.

These may also be projects that could add value to the property or make it more marketable like landscaping, updating the AC or hot water units, upgrading your electrical panel, or replacing sliders, doors, or windows.

ROI Projects

ROI (Return on Investment) projects are investments in your home, its marketability, and ability to create profit.

This category usually tends to overlap with the suggested projects, but the difference is that suggested projects are more focused on marketability and putting a buyer's mind at ease, whereas ROI is focused solely on increasing the buyer's perceived value.

For example, upgrading your AC isn't necessarily going to increase your home's value—it was already going to be valued at a certain price with the old unit.

However, when a buyer sees that the AC was just replaced last year, they are going to remove that from their list of potential expenses, saving you $5,000 in whatever they were planning on offering you.

However, when you upgrade your kitchen, you may have just added a $15,000 value to the home when compared to similar homes in the neighborhood that still have original kitchens or who haven't quite brought the kitchen up to date.

This update has just provided you with a profit, and while a kitchen remodel may not provide the best return on investment, later on in this chapter I've included some really simple ways to give your house a facelift and capitalize on your ROI.

These projects can vary, but the most common projects include replacing the AC and hot water units, upgrading kitchens and baths, replacing outdated flooring, and updating roofs, siding, or windows and doors.

The most important part of considering any ROI project is your recouped cost, so do some homework before you decide to take on a project.

With the advent of HGTV, many people want to upgrade their home to put it on the market with luxurious kitchens and baths, and while these will certainly add value to the home, they tend to cost more than is worth it in the end.

As I mentioned earlier, Cost vs. Value has a great website that updates the average costs for materials and labor, compares them to the recouped cost on a home's value or sale, breaking these stats down by state and zip code.

Prior to considering any estimates or quotes, do a little research on the projects you are considering. Talk about them with your agent to see if they will really be worth the cost and get estimates from contractors to compare to the research you gathered.

Cost Effective Upgrades and ROI Projects

There are also plenty of cost-effective ways to update and upgrade your home that will add a tremendous perceived value to buyers, at very little expense and effort to you. Some of the most common projects include:

- Landscaping the yard and garden beds

- Repainting the walls neutral colors or adding texture to walls and ceilings

- Upgrading hardware on doors, cabinets, and vanities

- Adding stone veneers to exterior walls as an accent to doors and windows

- Wrapping porch posts in aluminum or column wraps

- Replacing outdated appliances

- Upgrading bathroom vanities

- Updating lighting fixtures

- Painting doors and cabinets (professional painter)

- Replacing carpeted flooring with vinyl or composite flooring

- Replacing countertops with quartz, granite, or even stone-like composite countertops

Another great place to come up with some great DIY ideas or cost-effective facelifts is Pinterest. Say what you want about Pinterest, there are some awesome DIY home improvement and décor ideas.

These are just some of the things you may want to consider doing to your home, but the most important projects are by far the **required**, and I highly suggest doing them ahead of time, because most buyers are going to have an inspection done, and as we already covered, finding this out later costs money, time, and aggravation for both parties.

While you're still paying the taxes, utilities, a mortgage, and HOA fees, they're doing the same on their own home, condo, or apartment.

Best case scenario, they ask you for a credit back at closing to do the repairs on their own, but that means you may be leaving money on the table as well.

You're better off getting it all done ahead of time so there is no out for the buyer in the end, and the issue of losing money never comes up in the first place because you sealed the deal as soon as they made an offer with some good old-fashion proactivity.

Hiring Contractors to Prepare Your House

Once you've settled on the projects you need to take care of and have narrowed down the suggested and ROI projects, it's time to find the right people to do the work.

REALTOR Advantage – A Large Network

One of the best sources for finding good contractors and service providers is your listing agent. Good real estate agents have a large network of contractors, inspectors, lawyers, title companies, and lenders they work with on a regular basis and would be happy to match you up with.

I've included part of my own list of top-rated service companies in my own network in Appendix VIII.

The best may even be able to get you discounted rates on labor because they are feeding business to their network on a regular basis, so, don't be afraid to ask your agent who they recommend.

Angieslist.com is the "go-to" for many homeowners, and while I've never had to personally use it, I've heard excellent things from family and friends who have used it in the past. While you can join for free, they also offer membership upgrades for a nominal fee to simplify and manage the project as well as match you to highly rated contractors and sub-contractors.

Whether you use Angie's List or not, is up to you, but there are a few things you need to do to protect yourself and your home whenever you hire contractors.

First, do some research. Whether your agent provides you with some companies, or you find them on Google, do a thorough check-up. Look for their reviews on Google, social media, www.BBB.org, Yelp, and anywhere else you can think of.

Make sure you check your state's licensing website and see if their license is valid, their company is registered, and if they have any filings against them or judgement liens.

Next you will want to make sure there is a solid and thorough contract, including the following sections and clauses:

1. *A detailed job description best accompanied by an itemized work order and specific scope of work.* *(See Appendix IV)*

2. *Payment Terms with a specific payment schedule outlining the terms of subsequent payment releases.*

3. *Time of performance.*

4. *License and Status*

5. *Liability Waiver*

6. *Permits and Approvals*

7. *Liens and Waivers*

8. *Materials*

9. *Warranties*

10. *Dispute Resolution*

11. *Change Order*

12. *Not to Exceed Clause*

13. *Indemnification Clause*

14. *Site Maintenance*

15. *Seal/Signatures*

16. *Notice of Cancellation (Required by Federal Law)*

Make sure that your contractor will be using mechanical lien waivers, no matter how small the project. These not only protect the contractor for getting paid, but also protect you should the contractor ever come back and say that you didn't pay. They protect both sides.

I've included a Sample Contract in Appendix III as a reference. If you live in Southwest Florida, there's also a list of resources, and home-related service companies that I have worked with in the past who have done excellent work and come highly recommended.

Once these projects are completed, or as they are being completed, it's time to start laying out the blueprint for a quick and profitable sale.

Chapter 4 – Determining Your Price & Pricing Strategy

After only two days on the market Seller A received her first offer on the house. It was a bit lower than she would have liked, but seeing as how it had just been listed, she figured there would be plenty of better offers coming if it already caught people's attention this quickly.

Unfortunately, **statistics show that the first offer is most often the best offer and waiting on another offer on average costs the seller $10,000.**

Not only does waiting usually force sellers to accept less, it also costs them money having to sit on the market longer. Remember, you still must keep the house in good condition and keep up with the bills.

That's why pricing your home is one of the most crucial steps in the home selling process. But it's not enough to find the perfect listing price. You also need to have a pricing strategy—a system of adjusting your price with the market and timing.

The first three weeks of a new listing are when most of the activity will take place. *The graph below shows the average activity rate by time compiled from data over the years.*

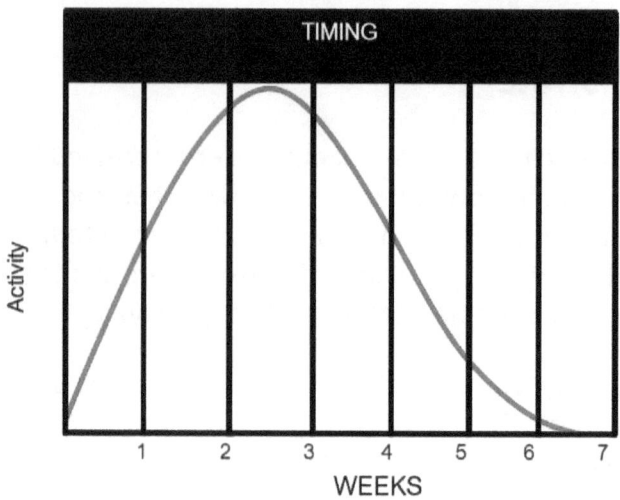

After the third week, the activity and interest steadily decline into weeks six and seven.

In general, the longer a home stays on the market, the more buyers will begin to think there is something wrong with it.

So how do you find your perfect price and how do you develop a pricing strategy?

Finding Your Perfect Price

My recommendation, especially if you are planning to sell the home on your own, is to get an appraiser to price the home for you. **Invest $200 or so on a third-party appraiser** to provide you with a market value price.

This was one of the investments we strongly recommended from our "Pre-Assurance Package." An appraiser will be able to provide you with a much more accurate market value price than you will be able to formulate on your own, and in many cases, more accurate than most agents'.

To be fair, there are many agents who are just as good at pricing homes, and many appraisers who ask agents to provide them with market data to help them formulate their appraisal, but the one advantage appraiser tend to have over agents, is that this is their job and if you find a good, local appraiser, they should be well aware of how much value a bedroom, garage, bathroom, pool, etc., adds or takes away from a home in your market.

So, is it better to overprice and hope you get offers for what you really want to sell it for, or should you underprice and hope for a bidding war?

Over or Under

While overpricing a home may seem like a good strategy in hopes that offers will come in near the price you want it to come in at, it tends to backfire. While over pricing your home is bad for obvious reasons, underpricing your home can be just as bad, leaving thousands of dollars on the table.

Once in a while underpricing may work in favor of the seller if they need to sell quickly, leading to a bidding war that usually ends fairly close to fair market value, however, I would encourage you to accept this as an exception to the rule.

Ideally you want to find the sweet spot for your home. The point at which your home draws a wide audience, but still provides you with a profit, or at least lets you breakeven.

But pricing to perfection is no easy feat. It's a bit of an art and requires a deep knowledge of the market and access to tools that most homeowners don't have access to.

REALTOR Advantage – CMA Tools & Skills

Realtors have access to several tools and databases that allow them to get a much deeper look at the market and provide you with a more accurate fair market value.

The MLS is a key tool, and while a homeowner may be able to list their home on an MLS for a flat fee (covered later in this book), they may not have the knowledge or skills to use the tools that will help them objectively and competitively price their home.

FSBO (For Sale by Owner) properties also sell for an average of 16% less than Realtor-Assisted transactions, which costs them much more than the 6% commission. You can read more on FSBO statistics at the National Association of Realtors website.

But how do you find the perfect price?

It comes down to analyzing certain data points in the MLS and being able to adjust the price of your home to several variables with similar homes. These variables include living area, bedrooms, bathrooms, building materials, location, features, age of the home, condition of the home, market trends and conditions, and many other variables.

Conducting A Simple CMA (Comparative Market Analysis)

If you've already had an appraiser or real estate agent do a CMA or appraisal for you as suggested in the beginning, you can skip this entire section.

Below I've laid out a very simple way of finding an approximate listing price.

The first thing you need to understand is the market. Is it a sellers' market or a buyers' market?

If you have access to the MLS, this can be analyzed through the market updates and statistics widget. However, if you don't have access to this tool, you could ask an agent, try finding it on YouTube, or use the Zillow market updates.

Zillow provides its users with market reports to keep up on the latest trends in the target market.

A buyers' market is when there is a large inventory of homes for sale and a much smaller number of buyers.

In this kind of market, homes can be purchased at a bargain because buyers have too many options to overpay for a home. This tends to drive prices down and houses will sit longer on the market.

A seller's market is when home inventory is low and there are many buyers still searching for homes.

At the time of this writing, Southwest Florida is in an extreme sellers' market, with most homes receiving multiple offers within the first couple weeks and driving prices up with bidding wars.

But it's not enough to know where the market is currently. You also need to understand where the market is heading, because **you want to "price ahead" of the market**.

If the market is currently a buyer's market, but the inventory is starting to drop, then it is trending towards a seller's market and you will be able to price your home a bit higher.

However, if a seller's market is starting to see more homes come on the market, you will unfortunately want to price your home a little lower than current fair market value so you won't be overpriced as the market turns and be forced to lower your price too soon.

Once you've determined the trend, you will need to look at **three different property statuses**: "Active," "Sold," and "Pending," and find homes that are at least similar in the **5 big categories—living area, number of beds, number of baths, location, and features**.

In other words, the homes you will be choosing from these 3 statuses should have a similar size, number of beds and baths, and comparable features, such as a pool, building materials, garage, etc. As a rule of thumb, you want these comparable homes, in all 3 categories, to be as close to your home as possible.

Prices can vary greatly from one neighborhood to the next, especially down here in Southwest Florida. Sometimes it can vary from one side of the street to the other. I've seen homes listed at $2M on one side of the street, and a modest $350K on the other. And if you know that is the case in your neighborhood, choose homes that have comparable priced land parcels.

"Active" properties are the homes that are currently on the market. These are homes that are listed for sale and have not sold yet. Actives will tell you what your competition will be, and I suggest studying these homes, looking at what separates your home from theirs, and using those differences to help market your own.

These homes are the ones you will have to compete with for attention from buyers, so find your homes strengths and highlight them.

"Sold" properties are homes that have recently sold no more than 6 months ago. The more recent the sale, the better the comparable, because it is more relative to the market you are currently in. Markets can change drastically within 6 months, so it's best to find sales as close to your present date as possible.

These homes will tell you what people actually paid for a home and will give you the best point of comparison for your own home and what it is likely to sell for.

"Pending" properties are homes that are currently on the market and are in escrow or under contract. These homes are the litmus-test for the current market and are another good source of data for coming up with a listing price.

The only problem with pending homes is that you don't know the price of the offer that was accepted. It could be $30K less than what they asked, or it could have sold over asking price.

What it does provide you is a listing price that was competitive enough or attractive enough to draw in buyers and ultimately an offer. The more similar these pending homes are to yours, the better your comp.

The DIY Method

Using these 3 points of data you can begin to adjust your home based on the features. For example, you may shave $10,000 off for your home only having 2 bedrooms as compared to a home that sold last week that had 3 bedrooms. You might reduce your price $15,000 for not having a garage or increase your price $25,000 for having a screened in pool and updated kitchen as compared to the active home 2 blocks down the street from you.

This is where an appraiser or experienced real estate agent can really come in handy. They are working with listings and home prices all the time and should know your market if they specialize in, or are familiar with, your area.

You can go on Zillow and see both sold, and active properties, but it can be a fickle source because you never really know when it updated its database last. Homes may have already been sold, or maybe under contract, and you won't know until you call the listing agent for more information.

If you get access to a flat-fee MLS, which I highly recommend doing, you'll have access to other tools and options to develop your listing price, such as "Pending" sales.

In the chapter on listing, I'll provide you with some flat-fee MLS sites you can use. I've also put together a simple video of me showing you how to use Zillow to do a CMA on your own. You can also find it by going to my YouTube channel. Just type in "Where To Live in Southwest Florida."

If you need to sell quickly, you might consider pricing a little lower than the price you came up with in hopes of creating a multiple offer situation that could lead to a bidding war and drive the price up, but at the very least will sell your home quickly. This tends to only work when it's a seller's market and your home has a highly desired location and features.

Once you've decided on a listing price, you need to determine your pricing strategy to adjust with the trends and time on the market, should it sit too long.

Determining Your Pricing Strategy

Every home and neighborhood is different—markets shift, and when they do, they can shift quickly.

Pricing adjustment strategies can vary, but the most frequently used is **the price drop**. You already know how this works. The home hasn't seen much action, the broker or agent tells his or her client it's time to drop the price, and upon doing so, they see a little increase in action.

This dance can go on forever sometimes, but usually happens because the home was priced too high to begin with or was priced behind the market trend.

This leads to buyer skepticism and usually a lower sale price.

Another pricing strategy is the **price increase**. This usually occurs when a home is withdrawn from the market for updates or repairs to be made. However that doesn't necessarily need to be the case. Sometimes increasing the price can intrigue buyers to want to look and see what caused the sudden increase.

A price increase without any significant updates or repairs obviously wouldn't be beneficial if you've had a lot of interest and action to begin with because those buyers who have already seen the property may be disappointed, but there are cases where this could benefit you if the market has shifted.

For example, let's say you had very little action in the first 3 weeks, so you increase the price for 1 week to stir the pot and get listed at the top again with a status change.

The following week you drop the price back to the original price, but now you haven't lost your profit margin, and on all of the search sites like Zillow and Realtor.com, it looks like you just made this huge drop in price.

The status change will send automatic emails to all the agents and clients in the MLS who have criteria that match your home, and it also signals to buyer that you want to make a deal and to bring offers.

The bottom line, a **price change** updates the database and puts your home at the top of the list again for status changes, so even something as small as a $100 price reduction slides you back into buyers inboxes.

Whatever your strategy, you want to have communicated it to your agent so you are both on the same page and will help each other stick to the strategy no matter what.

At last, you are ready to list it like a pro!

Chapter 5 – List It Like A Pro

In this chapter, I'm going to go through everything you need to set up your property and your listing for the best possible results.

This chapter is going to be dedicated to all the steps and resources you need to have in place to make the selling and closing process smooth and stress-free.

The next step in preparing your home for listing is getting the paperwork and documents ready.

Condos and Homeowners Associations

If you live in a condominium you will need to provide buyers with certain documents, at your own expense if you don't have them. The documents include the 1) **declaration of condominium, 2) articles of incorporation, 3) bylaws, 4) rules of the association, 5) most recent year-end financial information, and the 6) frequently asked questions and answers**.

If you live in a community with a **homeowner's association,** the only document you are required to provide the buyers with is a **disclosure summary** which includes information such as mandatory membership fees and assessments.

If you live in a condo that is inside an HOA community, you will need to provide both sets of documents.

Buyers are entitled to these documents and a **3-day review period** to cancel any offer without reason. This allows them the time to sift through the financials and documents and ensure they are purchasing a property that provides them with the terms they can live with.

In addition to these documents, the State of Florida is a "Duty to Disclose" state, meaning that you are required by law to disclose all information about the property's defects. A much simpler way of doing this is if you have already filled out a **Seller's Disclosure** and can provide potential buyers with copies of it.

You are not, however, required to provide buyer with this disclosure form, but you must disclose all defects in some form or another, so it might as well be on a disclosure form.

If you've done the pre-inspection and repairs you are golden.

Single-Family Homes

Single-family homes are generally a little more straight-forward, in that if it is not a part of a homeowner's association, the typical seller's disclosure, sale and purchase agreement, and any additional riders your property might require for your objectives, is all you may need.

Below is a brief list of some of the more common rider's and addendum your home might need:

Lead Paint Disclosure – For homes that were built pre-1978.

Defective Drywall Rider – For homes built between 2001 and 2009.

FIRPTA Rider – If you are a foreign investor.

Condominium Rider – For selling a condominium.

HOA Rider – For selling a home in a community with a Homeowners Association.

Getting the Forms

Because Florida real estate contracts are copyrighted and only licensed agents and lawyers can fill them out, there are 3 ways of getting these forms without a license:

1. You can hire a real estate agent to setup and fill out the paperwork, but this could cost you a flat fee or commission.

2. You can have a buyer's agent setup and fill out the paperwork, which you can negotiate into the 3% commission.

3. You can pay for a flat-fee MLS membership, which I would highly recommend anyways if you are selling your own property. Many times they will provide you with access to the documents you will need, and may have an additional package for getting an agent's help in filling out the forms.

Having a listing agent makes this process much simpler.

They already have access to all the forms, they will fill them out for you and know how to fill them out correctly so you don't find yourself in legal battles later on, and add an extra layer of legal protection from lawsuits.

In the contracts section coming up, I'll go over how contracts can be used to your advantage.

Knowing which forms to include in your deals is also another benefit.

Besides knowing if the Sale and Purchase agreement has been filled out correctly and you won't be getting taken to the cleaners, they can also help negotiate better terms for the sale, which you probably will not be able to do well if you don't understand the contracts fully.

If you are local to Southwest Florida, you can call or email me, and I'd be happy to help you get the documents setup at no cost.

Helping you gives me an opportunity to see your home first-hand, drum up buyers for you to sell to, and a chance that you might recommend me to other homeowners who are looking to buy or sell.

You will also want to choose a closing agent, which is most typically a lawyer or a title company. A title company assists in the transference of the property from the real property owner to the buyer. They also do a title search to find any issues with the deed and insure the transference for certain issues.

In most cases the seller chooses the closing agent, but there are instances when it is left up to the buyer or can be requested/negotiated into the terms of purchase.

You will need to speak with an attorney, agent, or title company to determine what the typical practice is in your community.

In the past, the closing agent may have been the brokerage itself, but nowadays it just isn't worth the liability for a brokerage to handle the money, so they will leave it up to the seller to choose the title company or lawyer they would like to handle the transaction and transference.

Contracts: "AS-IS" versus "Standard"

Unless you are a well-versed agent, or a real estate lawyer, you probably won't know the subtle differences between the "As-Is" contract and the "Standard" sale and purchase contracts. These subtle differences have **immense repercussions**.

While most agents today use the "As-Is" contract, in many cases, listing your home under the "Standard" contract is better.

The "Standard" doesn't have a whole lot of wiggle room for the buyer to get out of. Once a buyer puts an offer in under the standard contract, they must be committed and really want the home.

The only way out of the contract is if the buyer finds inspection issues, and they give you multiple opportunities to correct the problems. Other than that, there really isn't any way out for them unless you provide it.

In the "As-Is" contract the buyer is provided multiple ways to get out of the deal, one of which needs no explanation for walking away.

Therefore, having a great agent is more of an asset than a detriment, so you should seriously consider speaking to one or at the very least, a real estate lawyer.

Now it's time to begin the actual journey of setting up for your listing to go live online and public.

NOTE: *By this point you should have already had an inspection, repairs, appraisal, or CMA, determined your price point and pricing strategy, and have a general idea of your marketing plan.*

Home Staging

Over the last several years, home staging has gained an incredible amount of momentum and popularity in real estate.

What used to be considered a new construction staple and option for more luxurious homes has begun taking hold in every real estate market, from 1000 square foot homes to mansions.

After looking at the statistics, it's no surprise why.

Homes that were professionally staged sold 86% quicker than homes that were not staged and sold on average for at least 1% more money. In some cases it could be **as high as 3%,** which would completely negate the 3% commission you would pay an agent.

When you compare that to the average staging cost at $400, even in a small home the staging paid for itself and created a profit.

If you've ever been to a home that was professionally staged, you can certainly tell. It makes the room easier to envision living in, makes it seem well-worth the price, and can even tempt you to put an offer on something you might not even be able afford.

Empty homes make the home look smaller as well.

When deciding whether to have your home staged, it's not an all-or-nothing decision. Most companies have different staging packages you can purchase, and sometimes just purchasing items to stage your own home is enough in and of itself.

Compliments of Stage & Amaze, Fort Myers, FL

BEFORE PROFESSIONAL STAGING

AFTER PROFESSIONAL STAGING

If you think you are going to stage your own home, you can download a free consumer staging guide on the Real Estate Staging Association's website at Real Estate Staging Association.

You can also listen to an interview from my podcast with the company from these previous pictures. They are a local staging company who serves all of Southwest Florida and have won several awards for her work.

You can listen to the episode for more tips and answers to your questions at here.

Virtual Staging

Some other staging options include virtual staging. This is when a photographer or digital designer transposes virtual furniture and décor into a photo. It's like photoshop staging.

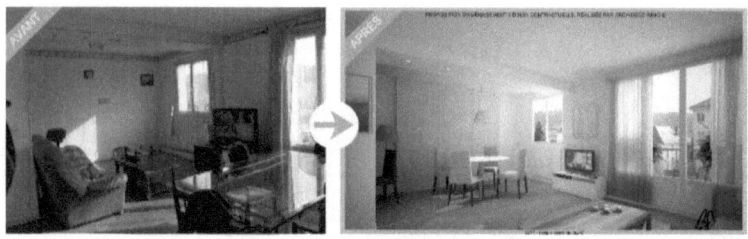

These services have really started popping up all over the place, but you need to be careful of who you choose to do this. There are many "designers" claiming to be able to virtually stage a home for a low price, but when you get the finished product, you can very easily tell that the photo was "photoshopped."

For good virtual staging companies, the prices are very reasonable starting at around $100 to stage an entire house, and increasing based on the number of photos, and size of the house.

This option works best for owners or investor who are on a budget and who are selling a vacant property. However, virtual staging can be used to touch up photos that have furniture in them as well. It all depends on what you want done.

Whatever you do, don't completely misrepresent the house by doctoring them too much. Buyer's and agents alike won't be happy if they show up for a tour and the home doesn't look like the photos at all.

DIY Staging

The third and most affordable option is staging your home yourself.

Staging a home doesn't have to be over-the-top. You can do some very simple things to your home that will change the entire atmosphere and feel of a room.

Doing things like getting a table cloth, or buying cheap plastic plates and silverware sets to set the table, as well as painting the walls different colors, changing out hardware in vanities and kitchen cabinets, or even having landscaping done outside to create a flattering curb appeal, can be very inexpensive and can make a huge difference.

Once your home is staged, you're ready to capture its beauty.

Hire A Professional Photographer

I highly recommend hiring a professional photographer.

With the technology and tools today, there is no reason not to invest a little in the photos. They can make a huge difference in the number of buyers who look at your home online and attract a few buyers to tour your home.

Not everyone has an eye for universal beauty though we all like to think that we do. Leave that stuff up to the professionals. You'll thank me later. Plus, you can get a good real estate photographer for around $300.

You don't need 30 photos, but you want enough of them to highlight the main living areas and some of the exterior features. And please, make sure there is an excellent shot of the front of the house from the road. **Buyers want to see the curb appeal, and if it's missing, they may just pass over it and move on.**

If its in a condo or community, include common areas and amenities too.

Before we get too far ahead of ourselves here, you need to make sure the home is presentable before you have your photos taken. These pictures are going to be what buyers see first, and if they see what this place looks like with someone else living in it, they can't picture themselves living in it.

While they may be an investment, they can really make a huge difference in what your home looks like online.

This means decluttering the home and removing personal items from sight. Clearing off countertops and minimizing artwork and décor to only the essentials. Too much décor can shrink a space and make it look too small in photos. Blinds should be opened, and shades drawn back to let as much natural light into the place as possible.

You want your place to look spotless as if you were having royalty over as guests.

Fancy Marketing Options

Some other options to consider, depending on the size, price point, and features of your home are the **3D Matterport** renderings, and **Video Tours**.

I recommend these options for homes that are at a higher price point, because while they do make the home more marketable, they are also an additional cost. These costs aren't necessary for smaller homes because it doesn't enhance the home enough to make it worth the cost.

You'll have to use your own judgement but usually a house that's under $250,000 may not be worth the additional investment for a For Sale By Owner.

3D Matterport renderings are those dollhouse images in which you can see a 3-dimensional layout of the floor plan. It looks just like a dollhouse with the walls being opened to show the interior walls of the room. You can also click on the rooms and it bring you down into them and let you walk around the house as if you are a doll within it.

Another thing to consider is getting a 3D tour done. This tour can include drone video but provides the buyers with a realistic walkthrough of the home to display its features and benefits in ways a photo cannot.

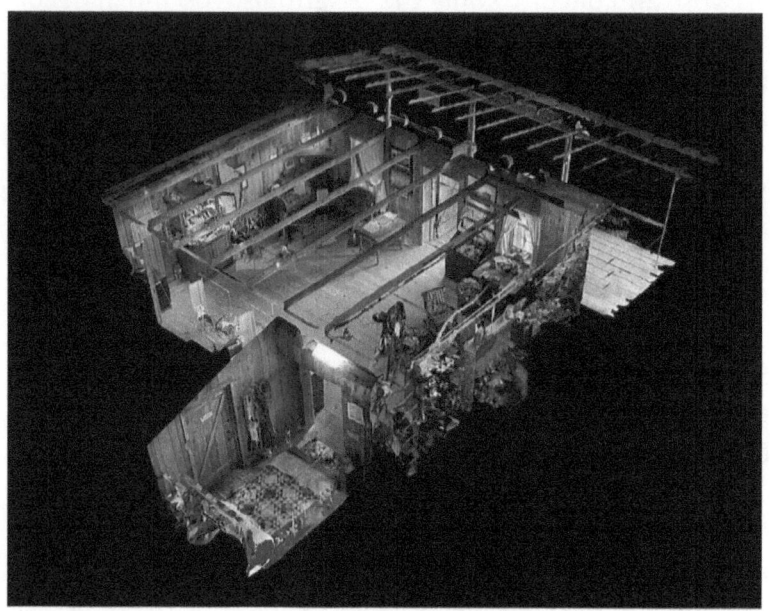

Matterport Dollhouse View

Most professional real estate photographers have the equipment and skills to do these types of renderings and videos as well and will have bundle packages that can save you money.

Make sure if your agent says that they include 3D tour videos of your home that they are actual videos and not just photo slideshows. Some agents call those slideshows 3D tours, but they are not the same.

Once you have your photography and videos done, you're ready to move onto writing a property description.

Crafting A Property Description

If you have an agent, they will complete all of this for you, but if you're doing this on your own, I've created a really straightforward guide to walk you through creating an elegant property description.

Part 1 - Key Highlight(s) & Location *(1-2 Standout Sentences)*

The first sentence or two should highlight what your ideal buyer is looking for, preferably something hard to find in the market and may draw attention to the location.

EX: *Stunning 3,121 square foot home on a quiet street in the highly desirous community of Hummingbird Cove makes this the largest home listed under $145/sq. ft.*

Part 2 - Property & House Basic Information *(2-3 Sentences)*

The next couple of sentences should speak about the basic information of the house, like the beds, baths, square footage, but should make the prospect want to read on to find out more.

EX: *With an incredible 4 bedrooms plus a den and 3.5 bathrooms, 18" tile throughout located on one of Cape Coral's gulf-access canals, this waterfront home will sell fast. Being in one of the most desired locations of the SW Cape, you won't believe what you're getting for the value.*

Part 3 - Features & Recent Upgrades *(2-4 Sentences)*

The next few sentences are where you capture the buyer. These sentences should hammer home the features and benefits that only this home can provide a buyer. Use your avatar profile to elaborate on your home in a way that entices the buyer to schedule a showing.

EX: *This home features a large screened in pool with a picture window lanai overlooking your 10,000 lb. boat lift and dock. The canal is just a 5-minute drive to the Caloosahatchee River, so you're never too far from escaping land and enjoying a sunset cruise. With a recently upgraded kitchen, including quartz countertops, premium grade cabinets, and a brand-new set of high-end stainless-steel appliances, you'll wow friends and family as you entertain from the kitchen out to the patio.*

Part 4 - Call to Action *(1-2 Sentences)*

The last sentence or two is where you give a call to action and can even sweeten the deal with an enticing offer if you'd like.

EX: *So, if you're ready to carve out your piece of paradise, schedule a tour this week to get a $1000 credit-back towards new flooring, or stop by our open house to learn more about this offer.*

Part 5 – Put It All Together

Put these sentences together into one paragraph. Don't be afraid to make certain phrases and words all capital letters or add symbols to draw attention to certain parts of the description.

Note: If you will be adding this to an MLS, you will not be able to include any contact information in the description. You may also want to check the fair-housing guidelines for what you can and cannot say about a property. There are tons of discrimination laws that dictate what can and cannot be said about a property.

Below is a list of some of the top keywords that helped sell homes as found by www.point2homes.com in a study of 300,000 listings. Many of these words can be sprinkled in your description to make it more attractive and elegant.

- Beautiful
- Hardwood floors
- Stainless steel appliances
- Renovated
- Private
- Spacious
- Closet space
- Brand new
- Luxury
- High ceilings
- Quiet
- Pool
- Granite countertops
- Perfect
- Must see
- Soaking tub
- Stunning
- Open kitchen
- Pet friendly

Securing Your Home for Showings

Prior to publishing your listing on the MLS, you'll need to figure out how you are going to coordinate showings and secure your home while making it accessible to other agents.

If you're listing your own home, you can go to most hardware stores or a Home Depot and get a door-handle key-box for around $30. You'll need to provide the instructions for access in the private notes section for agents to access the home.

You will also need to specify that they call you with a minimum notice time prior to showing so you can plan to be elsewhere, and I highly recommend being elsewhere.

A buyer wants to feel free to walk around and speak with their agent or family about the home, and they aren't going to feel comfortable doing that with you there.

Buyers like to take their time and envision themselves living there or where they would put their furniture to make the space work for them. They like to discuss what changes they would make or how they would update the home. All these things disappear when the homeowner is on the premises. I've seen this happen enough to be able to speak to it.

Most agents nowadays used what's called a Supra padlock. That is the digital padlock that can only be accessed by an agent who has remote access through the Supra system via smartphone. For that reason, **Supra's are a much more secure means of providing access to agents and their clients**.

The Supra system requires a real estate agent to be a member of an MLS or Realtor board.

What's nice about the Supra is that anytime an agent schedules a showing, as soon as the key is accessed that information is logged into a system. **It records who the agent was, what time they accessed the key, and when they put the key back,** signaling the ending of the showing.

After the showing, your agent has all that information to be able to follow-up with the agent and get feedback, or just use the data to see how long people are staying for the showing.

Generally, a longer showing shows that a buyer is considering the property and mulling over the details and whether it will work for them.

The other nice thing about the Supra system is that **at the end of the showing it will ask the agent to provide feedback for both themselves and their client as to how the showing went.** It will send out this automatic feedback request 3 days in a row if they have not completed it, which provides a greater chance of getting feedback.

This information is gold because it will ask how the agent and buyer felt about the price point, the showing itself, and any other questions you would like to manually add into the survey.

Turnkey or Unfurnished

Selling a home "turnkey" or fully furnished adds a nice value to the property but can be tricky if the buyer is using financing. Most title companies and lawyers will ask that the furniture be sold as a separate bill of sale and not included in the contract because of how complicated it can make the financing portion of the contract.

Publishing Your Home to the MLS

While there are plenty of FSBOs who choose not to use the flat-fee MLS systems, I would encourage you to do so. It lets your home reach the widest audience possible by including it not only in the local MLS for buyer's agents to see, but also will add you to the major search sites like Zillow, Realtor.com, Homes.com, Redfin, and many others.

While it will be a few hundred-dollar investment, it is well-worth the price. Listing it in the MLS is what makes it so easy for home buyers to find your home when an agent lists it there. Why wouldn't you use the same tool?

These are a couple sites you can use to list your home for sale in the MLS at a flat rate:

http://www.snapflatfee.com/florida/mls

http://www.brokerlessmls.com

http://www.listwithfreedom.com/florida

http://www.brokerdirectmls.com

http://www.unlimitedmls.com/

You can also try FSBO websites like:

https://www.houzeo.com

https://www.forsalebyowner.com

https://www.fsbo.com

Despite the investment, it will make your life a lot easier if something needs to be changed, or your home sells. Everyone will get the updates in real time rather than waiting for the major sites to update.

Once in the MLS, you will need to fill in the property details, the property description, showing instructions, any pertinent agent information, and upload the photos. **Please make sure the photos are positioned correctly in the MLS.**

Now you're ready to start creating your marketing materials and follow through on your plan.

Chapter 6 – Marketing Like A Pro

If you're working with an agent, you should have done your due diligence already and be familiar with your agents marketing reach, as well as the kinds of tools and strategies they will be using to market your home.

If on the other hand, you are marketing your own home, this chapter is going to give you all the materials and step-by-step directions to market like a professional.

FREE Ads and Marketing

Besides using the flat-fee MLS to get your house on all the listing sites, there are also several ways you can market your home for free.

Two of the most popular places to post home listings for free are Facebook Marketplace and Craigslist. Both websites have a huge reach and are used daily to search for homes.

In fact, in our brokerage **Craigslist** and **Facebook Marketplace** are one of the top ways that many new agents list their homes for their clients and try to develop buyer leads.

While Facebook Marketplace is straightforward, I will walk you through the steps to the basic steps to list a property.

Facebook Marketplace

*As of this writing, you'll have to **list your property from your phone** if you are using the new version of Facebook.*

Step 1

From your Facebook app, click the pancake menu button in the bottom right corner of your phone. From the list, choose "Marketplace."

Step 2

In the top left, under the search bar, choose the "sell" button.

Step 3

Choose "Homes for Sale or Rent" from the bottom pop-up menu.

Step 4

From this screen fill out the information for your home, upload pictures, and make sure you choose "Homes for sale" under the category selection menu.

Step 5

Continue filling out as much information as you can and then publish the post to the marketplace.

Craigslist

As for Craigslist, there are several steps to creating your Craigslist ad and I walk you through them below.

Step 1

If you don't already have one, you'll need to create an account. Once you've created your account, on the home page, you'll need to click on the "create a posting" link underneath "Craigslist" in the top left corner of the page.

Step 2

Choose your county or region.

choose the location that fits best:

- ○ lee county
- ○ charlotte county
- ○ collier county

please note: your posting will also appear on the main **ft myers / SW florida** site.

continue

Step 3

Choose "housing offered"

please limit each posting to a single area and category, once per 48 hours

what type of posting is this: (see prohibited list before posting.)

- ○ job offered
- ○ gig offered (I'm hiring for a short-term, small or odd job)
- ○ resume / job wanted

- ○ housing offered
- ○ housing wanted

- ○ for sale by owner
- ○ for sale by dealer
- ○ wanted by owner
- ○ wanted by dealer

- ○ service offered

- ○ community
- ○ event / class

continue

Step 4

Choose "real estate – by owner"

please choose a category: (see <u>prohibited</u> list before posting.)

○ rooms & shares
○ apartments / housing for rent (no shares, roommates, or sublets please!)
○ housing swap
○ office & commercial ($5 per post)
○ parking & storage
○ real estate - by broker
○ real estate - by owner
○ sublets & temporary
○ vacation rentals
○ wanted: apts
○ wanted: real estate
○ wanted: room/share
○ wanted: sublet/temp

[continue]

Step 5

Fill out the form as completely as possible. As a trick for the "posting title," put the bathrooms first as in the picture (below). When you publish the post, the baths will be shown right after the beds in the title, so it looks complete. Fill out the description with the description you created in the property description template.

posting title	city or neighborhood	postal code
2ba + Den Luxurious Pool Home on Gulf-Access	Whiskey Creek	33919

description

posting details

price	housing type	☐ furnished	available on
$ 349000	house	☐ no smoking	select date
sqft	laundry	☐ wheelchair accessible	open house dates
2143	w/d in unit	☐ EV charging	
	parking		
	attached garage		
	bedrooms		
	3		
	bathrooms		
	2		

Step 6

Put in the email you'd like to be notified at of any interest.
If you're comfortable with giving out your number, you
can put that into your property description on a separate
line at the bottom. Callers are generally the most invested
in their search.

bedrooms
3

bathrooms
2

contact info

email
jsmith@home.com

email privacy options [2]
- CL mail relay (recommended)
- no replies to this email

phone/text
- show my phone number   phone calls OK   text/sms OK

phone number   extension   contact name

location info
- show my address

street   cross street   city

- ok for others to contact you about other services, products or commercial interests

continue

Step 7

I would recommend keeping your address off Craigslist, not only for safety reasons, but also, if you give buyers everything they need, there is no reason for the ad or them contacting you—they can drive and see it on their own.

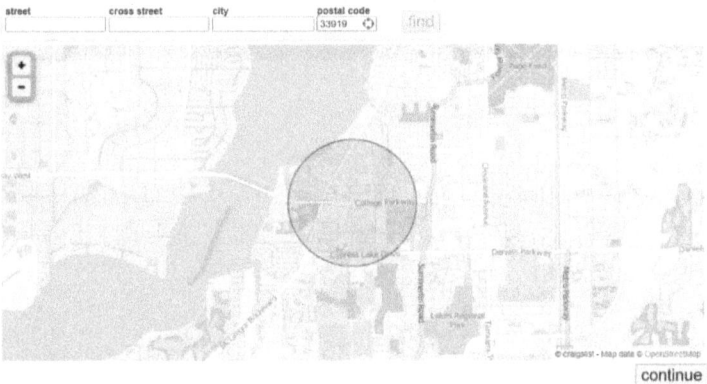

Step 8

As with the properties address, I would put up the best and most appealing pictures for the property but wouldn't spend time putting all the pictures up. Again, there would be no reason for them to contact you.

Step 9

Once you have completed these steps you can hit
"publish" on the following screen, but you're not done yet.
You'll receive an email that asks you to confirm that you
want to publish the ad. In that email you will need to click
the link, and then accept the terms to publish it to the site.

Next, I usually schedule a broker's open house for my
clients, and a Pro Open House for buyers.

Hosting an Open House

Now, without any breaks you should investigate setting up
an open house. This is going to require some time and
effort in setting up flyers and brochures, ordering street
and yard signs, as well as posting ads and events about it
on social media, the newspapers, and other classifieds.

If you had the professionals do the photography and
videos make sure you have copies of those saved on your
computer for you to upload to websites like Facebook and
Craigslist.

One of the number one tools I always recommend to people for digital design work is Canva because it makes the design and editing process simple enough for anyone to be able to do it.

I've taken the liberty to already design a brochure for you below. All you must do is click the link underneath it, swap out the photos, and change the text in the template.

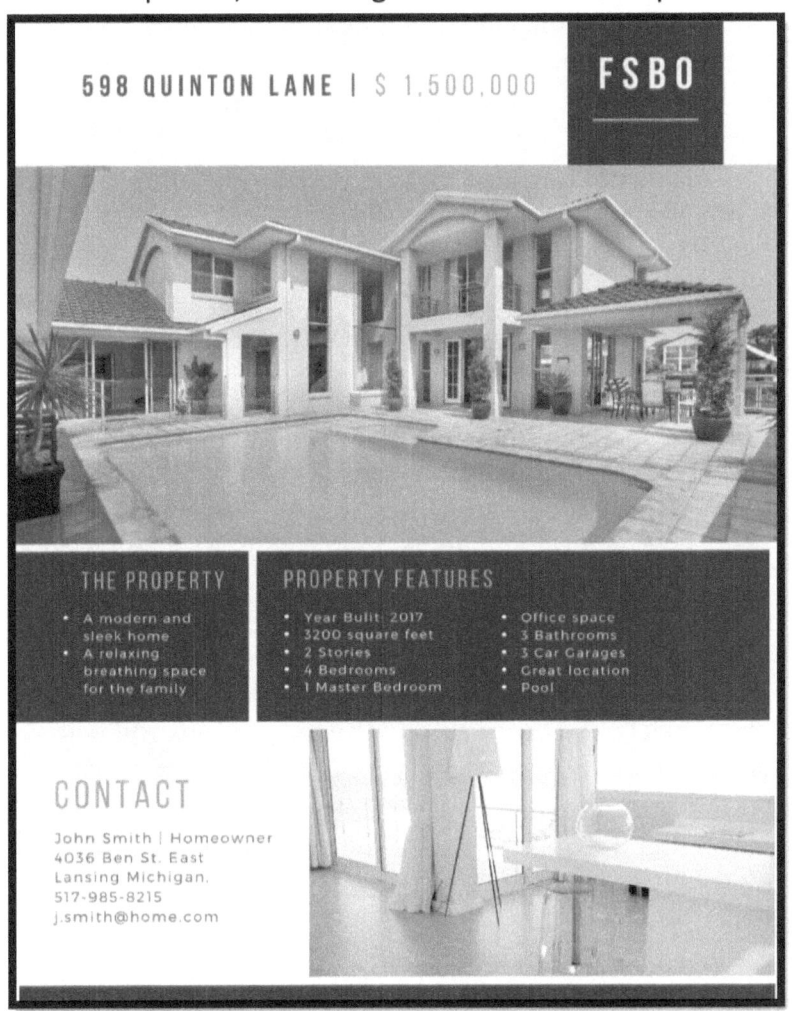

Download this Template to customize the pictures and text for your home.

This brochure is perfect for handing prospective buyers at the open house or casing the neighborhood with them and local businesses.

Canva is also great if you're going to be creating online ads through Facebook, Instagram, or even YouTube. You will want your thumbnail photos and any marketing materials that you use in them to be high quality and that's where Canva shines.

It has an entire portfolio of templates for every shape, size, and platform, and all you must do is change out the pictures and text—then hit print.

The Pro Open House

While you may not necessarily be able to host a broker's open house, you can host a regular open house with a twist—what I call a "Pro Open House." Read through the steps first, and then begin implementing the plan.

Step 1 – Choose an Open House Date

Ideally you will want the open house date to be within the first week of the home hitting the market, but you will want to give yourself at the very least 3 days to prepare. (There is some work to be done and some time needed for marketing the open house to reach the most amount of people).

Besides choosing a date, you may also consider choosing the time. Sometime showings can highlight a home's features better at night with the right lighting and can make an excellent cocktail party. This will all depend on your price point and your target audience.

Step 2 - Scout Out the Neighborhood

Take a drive around the neighborhood and locate the main roads and multiple pathways a prospect could take to get to the home. Identify yards and intersections that would be ideal to place open house signs.

Ask those neighbors if they mind you putting your signs on their yard temporarily.

Step 3 – Research Local Ordinances

While you want to market the property as soon as possible, you'll need to check with local ordinances to see if you are legally able to place signs in public areas such as medians and street corners. You will also need to find out what the time allowance is on such placements.

Step 4 – Neighborhood Outreach

I'm no fan of door-knocking, but when it comes to hosting an open-house, this is one time where I don't mind it. Neighbors tend to be the greatest advocates of your neighborhood so they will naturally brag about your neighborhood to friends, family, and anyone they meet that is looking for a home.

Invite them and anyone else they know to stop by for the open house.

Step 5 – Marketing

Whether you are an agent listing a home, or you're the homeowner, you are going to want to market the open house in as many places as possible. If you have access to the MLS through a Flat-Fee MLS or as an agent, that is one of the key areas to market it.

Classifieds, like Craigslist and other local news sites, is another great place to market them. You can even post them on Facebook Marketplace or create Facebook ads for it to reach more and more people.

REALTOR Advantage – Advanced Marketing Platforms

One of the top marketing tools that we use in our brokerage is called Listings2Leads. It's for Realtors and can costs hundreds of dollars to purchase on your own, but it allows us to do some incredible things for marketing your property.

Once we add your home to the system, it will automatically create a ton of marketing materials, both printable and digital like brochures, postcards, single page websites, social media posts, and ads that can be posted to virtually every social media platform.

Whenever someone clicks on the digital posts, whether it's a landing page, ad, or social media post, it will direct the prospect to a custom landing page for your property where it will capture their contact information from social media, or from them manually entering it.

With a Facebook sign-in, most of the leads we get provide us with their real contact information because it is collected from Facebook.

This allows us to create buyer leads and follow up on those

leads to get buyers interested in your home. It's an incredible tool for real estate marketing!

Step 6 – Prepare for The Open House

Two key materials you will want to have prepared are the Property Brochure to hand out to buyers, and a sign-in sheet. You can use the brochure template I provided earlier for this. You can also sign up for an account on Canva and browse through the flyer templates they have.

The sign in sheet is the most important. This provides you with contact information so you or your agent can follow up with anyone who took the time to come to your open house. You can ask them for feedback on the price, the condition, the location, and any other information that may be valuable in making future decisions on the listing. Just let them all know you would like them to sign in for the safety of your home and valuables.

If you have an agent, let them use you as the reason to have guests sign in. If guests have an agent, the agent may sign in for their customers instead and you can contact them to follow-up.

Step 7 – Host It and Follow Up

The final step is to host the open house.

Depending on your price point, you may consider providing beverages and light snacks for your guests.

During the event, offer to answer guests' questions about the home and handout the brochures. Be careful not to disclose information that you are uncertain of. If you don't know the answer to a question, you are better off saying you don't know and taking down their information if you haven't already got it on the sign-in sheet.

Find out the answer from a professional and get back to them later.

After the guests leave, make sure you follow up with them via email, text, or phone call. I wouldn't wait too long to follow up. Even a full day later may be too long and they may already have forgotten your home. Send them a text first explaining who you are and ask if they have a few minutes to chat.

If they don't answer within an hour, give them a call. Ask them for feedback using the questions below.

If they answer, follow up with an email thanking them for their time and feedback. If they don't, send them an email asking them the questions instead.

Feedback Questions

1. What did you think of the home?

2. How did you feel about the neighborhood?

3. What initially interested you in the property?

4. How did you feel about the asking price?

5. What did you like most about the home?

6. What did you like least about the home?

7. Is this home one that you are considering making an offer on?

8. Do you have any other questions I can help answer?

One of the nice things about the brokerage I work for, MVP Realty, is that any agent in the brokerage can market and advertise any other agent's listing within our own brokerage.

For example, if I list your house, all MVP agents statewide, can also pull your listing and create ads to market it.

Why would they want to do that?

Because it gives them something to market that will draw in buyer leads for them to work with.

So besides me having **over 800 other agents and their clients that I can market your listing to, you have 800 other agents who can potentially market your home as well**. It creates a compound marketing effect.

Paid Ads

There are many places to take out paid ads, but the most cost-effective today are still social media ads.

In this section I will show you how to create a Facebook ad, because I have found Facebook ads to still be one of the most cost-effective places to generate leads as a Realtor.

Follow these step-by-step instructions on creating a Facebook Ad, and you'll be marketing just like a professional.

Facebook & Instagram Ads

First let's breakdown the dynamics of a Facebook and Instagram ad. There are 3 main sections to an ad, and each one plays a key role in developing the audience's interest enough to click on the link.

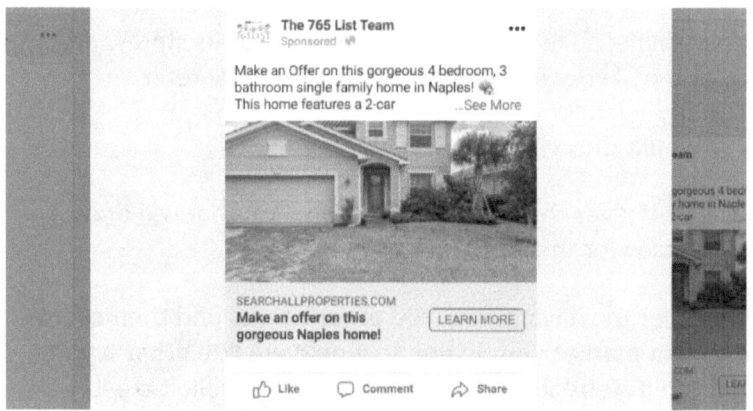

1 – The Picture

Audience will look at the picture first. The picture is the most important part of the ad and must catch the audience's eye.

2 – The Headline

Next the audience will look at the title below the picture. This needs to be something that will intrigue the prospect and make them want to read the description.

3 – The Description

Finally, the description at the top should give them just enough information to want to learn more and act by clicking the button.

Facebook Desktop Ad

Instagram Ad

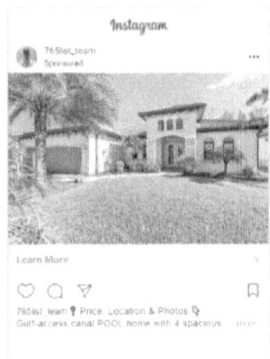

Creating A Facebook Ad

Step 1

From your Facebook home page, click the plus sign in the upper right-hand corner and choose "Ad" from the drop-down menu. This is what will show.

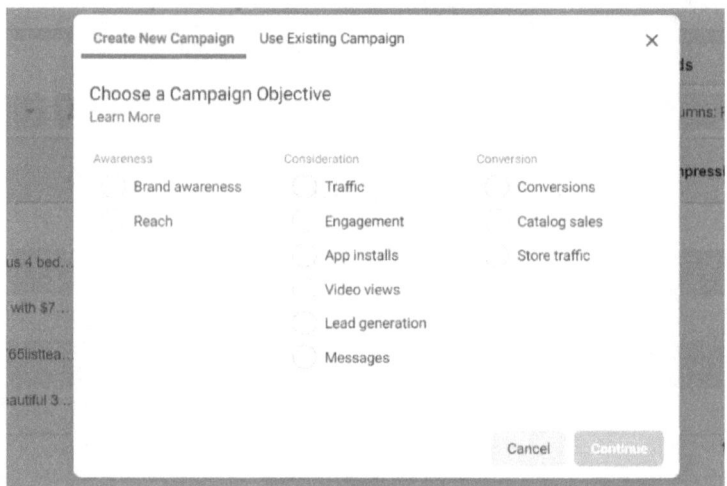

Step 2

Choose the objective you feel most comfortable following up with leads. **Traffic** focuses on quantity and can direct leads to websites, messenger, and more. **Lead generation** will ask the lead to fill out a form with contact info, so you'll get less leads, but they'll be higher quality. **Conversions** will show the ad to people who are further in their search but will provide the least amount of leads.

Step 3

You can name these different levels whatever you'd like or leave them blank, but if you plan on creating several campaigns or investing in real estate regularly, you'll want to title them according to their differences. "Campaigns" titles are specific to the purpose of your ad. "Ad Sets" are specific to your audience and location. The "Ad" is important to label only if you plan on using multiple ads within an "Ad Set" or "Campaign."

Step 4

Once you've chosen your titles, you will need to toggle the Special Ad Categories and choose "Housing" as Facebook now regulates several special ad categories. If you don't toggle this, your ad will not be approved.

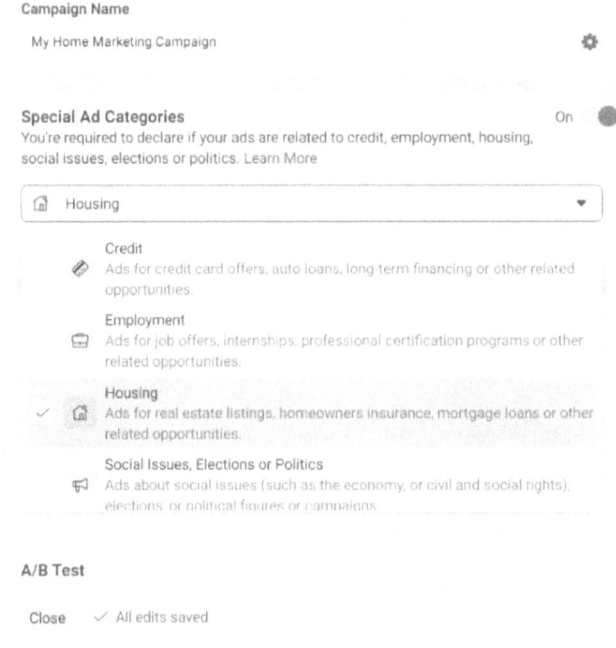

Step 5

Once you've chosen the special ads category, you can skip the A/B testing. This is a more advanced marketing tool that allows you to test multiple ads or ad variables to see which is performing the best.

Next choose your budget. You can choose a daily budget if you plan to run it continuously, or a lifetime budget if you have a set amount you want to spend and that's it.

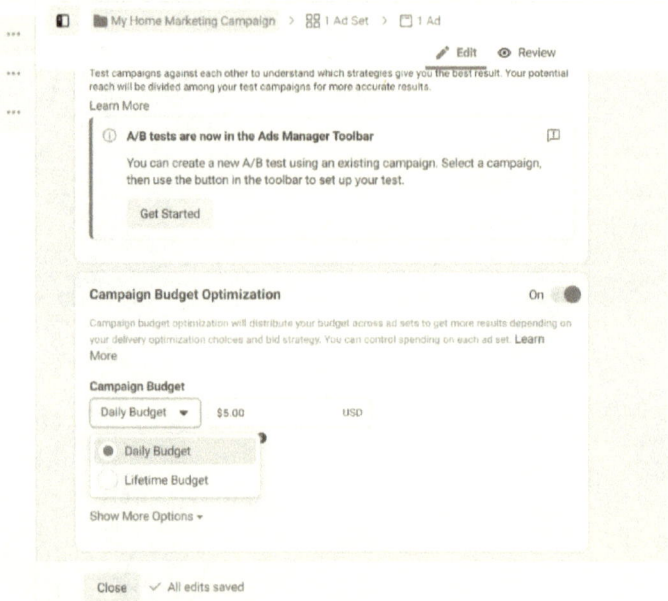

Step 6

As you scroll down the page further, you'll see options for where you want your traffic to be directed. Each option presents its own set of unique pros and cons. Put yourself in a lead's shoes and weigh which one you'd be most likely to act on. Each one has a certain level of anonymity to it.

The **Website** option provides you with the most room to direct your audience exactly where you want them to go, like a landing page, which you can easily create on Weebly for free. It also doesn't necessarily require the lead giving you any personal information.

The **App**, **Messenger**, and **WhatsApp** choices require the lead to provide their information because they are directly connected to Facebook.

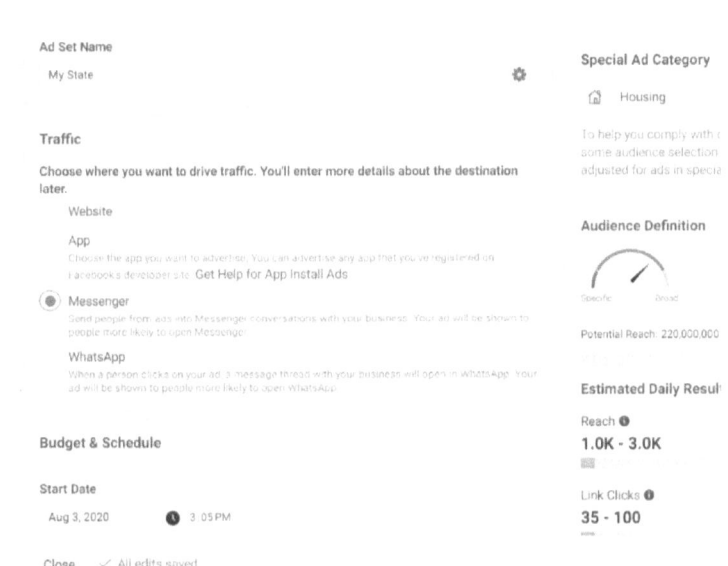

Step 7

As you scroll further down, you'll see the section for choosing your audience. You don't need to create anything or change anything for that matter unless you are creating more advanced ads. The only things you will need to change are adding in your location...

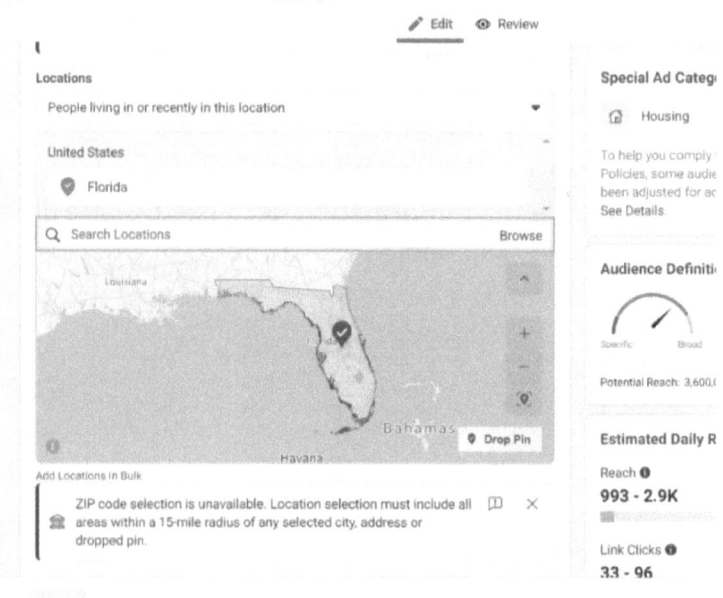

... and adding in your audience's interest. Facebook pulls data from cookies left behind by other websites and can pinpoint people who have visited certain sites or have certain interests. For your ad, **there are only 5 interests you need to target...Zillow, Homes.com, Realtor.com, Housing.com, and Trulia.**

Why? Because these are the sites buyers will be visiting recently that would be your best audience. Then click Next.

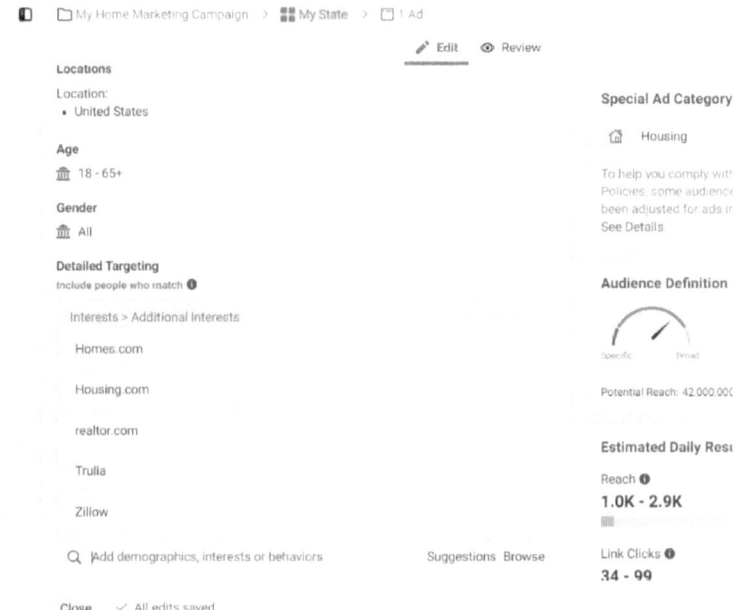

Step 8

Now you're ready to start creating your ad. The most important part of the ad is choosing a picture that pops and will draw attention. If you fail here, the ad is as good as dead. The second thing people will look to next if they like the picture is the Headline (the gray box). This needs to be enticing for the lead to want to read or learn more.

Lastly, the audience, if still intrigued by the picture and headline, will look to the paragraph at the top or "Primary Text" to read the rest. The primary text is where you should explain a little more to entice the audience just enough to act and click on the add or button. See a couple examples below on how you can setup your ads for a good CTR or click-through rate.

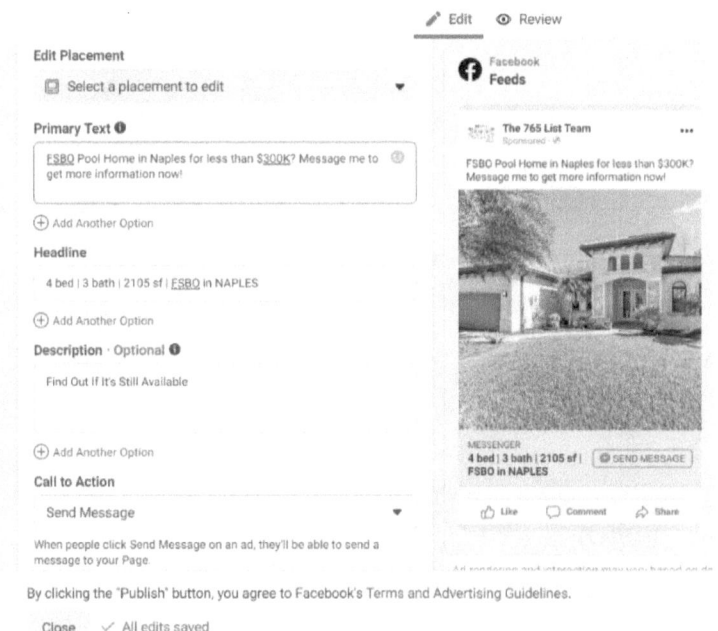

Finished Products

Learn More Ad on Facebook

How Can You Help If You Have An Agent?

Even if you hired an agent to market your home, there are a few ways you can still help them make the selling process smooth and easy.

1. Have things to do, people to see, or places you can visit ready while your home is on the market, so you can be flexible with showings.

2. You can also help the agent by posting your listing to your social media platforms and talking it up to everyone you meet.

3. It's also best to keep your home as clean as possible. There's nothing worse than having beautiful pictures online that draw buyers in, only to disappoint them at the actual showing.

   Buyers want to see a clean, decluttered space that they can envision putting their own finishing touches on and putting their own furniture and style into.

4. The final suggestion is to follow-through with your pricing strategy. After that three-week window anybody who is already in the market will have already considered your home and moved on from it.

From then on, the people considering your home will either be just entering the market or looking for a deal—and it won't be in your favor. Revisit the pricing strategy section in Chapter 4 if you need to.

Chapter 7 – Receiving Offers

If you've taken my advice on getting our "Pre-Assurance" package done, and have had your home inspected, repaired, and appraised, you won't have to worry about much in this section. Still, there are some scenarios worth understanding as you begin receiving offers.

One of the main things to understand as you start to receive offers is that the statistics generally show that the first offer, is usually the best.

I don't say that to discourage you, but I do hope that it will be something you seriously consider before passing on an early offer that isn't exactly what you want.

As homeowners, we all tend to overvalue our home for a few different reasons. It's natural and we almost all do it, even if we're an agent.

We know its potential, we know and love all the quirks we've grown partial to over the years, and we've built memories we will never forget there. But those are intangible values that don't translate to other's lives.

Too often, homeowners sabotage themselves by passing on a reasonable offer because they are either not ready to part with their home fully, or they have given it more value than the current market is willing to offer for it.

What's A Good Offer?

That's a fair question, however, **it will really depend upon the market**.

As we discussed earlier in the book, you need to understand where the market is heading. If it has shifted or is starting to shift towards a seller's market, you may be able to wait for a better offer and may be able to demand an offer closer to your asking price.

If the market has shifted to a buyer's market, you will probably need to be a little more flexible in your consideration.

If you're working with an agent, you can ask him to run another CMA for as many homes as possible that are **similar in size, rooms, and area**, that have *sold in your area over the last 3-6 months.*

If you're not working with an agent, you should be able to do the same thing in your flat fee MLS or find some of this information on Zillow under the "Sold" filter.

The CMA will be able to tell you what the original asking prices were, how long they were on the market before getting sold, and what the sold prices were for the comps.

If you have enough data points on the CMA, you will be able to figure out the average sale price percentage when compared to the asking price.

If the CMA doesn't automatically do this for you, simply add all the asking prices together and divide by the number of homes. Then add all the sold prices together and divide by the number of homes. Now divide the sold price average by the asking price average.

The decimal you are left with is the average percentage of the asking price that homes sold for. Move the decimal point 2 numbers to the right and that is the percentage. This will give you a realistic idea of what a decent offer will fall around according to the market.

Example

Homes	Asking Price	Days on Market	Selling Price
1	$289,000	13	$282,000
2	$350,000	65	$339,800
3	$274,900	134	$250,000
4	$304,900	55	$295,000
Average	$304,700	66.75	$291,700

In the example above, the average selling price of the 4 homes was $291,700 and the average asking price was $304,700, giving us an average sale percentage of 95% of the asking price.

For this market, you can expect to stay on the market for an average of 66 days and receive an offer of 95% of your asking price.

Now let's break down the homes and what might have happened just based on these numbers.

Home 1

Home number 1 sold in 13 days around the median price range. It was sold for 97% of the asking price. 13 days is a quick turnaround and getting 97% of asking price tells us that this home was priced aggressively. It was low enough to attract offers quickly that were close to what it was asking, which shows us that it might have been one of the best priced homes in the market at the time.

This house probably could have gotten more than it received, but the owner and agent obviously felt that this was a good offer and took it. The alternative could have been waiting 2 months like house number 2 and 4, which would have cost an additional 2 months in mortgage payments, HOA fees, taxes, utilities, all which could have added up to another $3,000, and there was no guarantee that a better offer was coming. If it had an offer within the first 3 days, it might have been worth waiting for another offer, but nothing is guaranteed.

Home 2

Home number 2 was on the market for 2 months but also received 97% of its asking price. This home might have been priced well for what it offered, but it might have been one of the largest houses in the neighborhood, in which case most people feel they should never buy the biggest home in the neighborhood because you have capped your resale value.

Home 3

Home number 3 was the lowest priced home in this grouping but was also on the market for 134 days and eventually sold for 90% of its asking price. By the numbers this home, despite being the lowest price, was overpriced for the market and most likely for its condition. This home may have had inspection issues, may have been a foreclosure, and was most likely not kept in good condition.

Home 4

Home number 4 is like home number 2 in that it sold for around 97% of its asking price in 55 days meaning it was around the median for value versus price. It wasn't the lowest priced and didn't offer the best value most likely as far as features are concerned, but it was priced well and with the right buyer sold within 2 months.

Financing Contingencies

Contingencies, financing, and other additional terms in an offer are something you will really want to sit down and think about.

Each one can have a major impact on the amount of time, money, and effort the closing period is going to require. Each one is also a potential delay or cancellation of the deal.

Early in the book we had discussed VA Loans as a one such financing option that you should do some research on because it may require you to pay additional fees for the buyer.

FHA loans are also another financing option that has some strict rules when it comes to the kind of house and condition that is allowable for its program.

A financing contingency is one of the most common, even if it isn't for an FHA/VA loan, and gives the buyers a way out of the contract if they can't get fully approved for financing. This tends to happen if a buyer has withheld information in their pre-qualification or pre-approval process, or after getting the pre-approval letter, has made financial decisions that has now affected their credit or ability to receive financing.

The best protection you have against this happening is to require a "Loan Estimate," or "proof of funds."

Most agents ask for a "pre-approval letter," however, pre-approval letters aren't worth anything nowadays. Make sure to specify that a "pre-approval" and "pre-qualification" letter will not suffice.

The main difference between a pre-qualification letter and a pre-approval letter is that the pre-qualification is based on a lender asking a few questions of the buyer and basing their qualification on those answers and a little bit of digging into their financials.

A pre-approval letter requires the lender to do a little more due diligence in vetting the buyer.

Only a **"Loan Estimate"** will require the lender to do a deep-dive into a buyer's credit-report and essentially underwrite the loan ahead of time. This kind of buyer is more serious and invested in the home-buying process.

You can also request a minimum amount or percentage of earnest money to be deposited with a buyers offer in order for it to be considered.

It isn't typical, and will reduce your potential buyers pool, but it will also weed out the tire-kickers. It is worth considering that there are many first-time homebuyers that may not be able to meet these requests.

Other Contingencies

Buyers can choose to include other contingencies that I mentioned earlier as well, such as an inspection contingency, appraisal contingency, or a contingency that the buyer's home must sell first.

REALTOR Advantage – Where Agents Shine

Having a great Realtor, or lawyer, can really pay off when it comes time to negotiate contracts and make decisions on offers.

If your lawyer or agent are familiar with contracts, they can negotiate a deal in your favor without the other Realtor or agent knowing what is even going on.

Surprisingly, there are a relatively large number of agents who don't know how to use contracts to better position their clients and negotiate better terms for their deals.

Each of these contingencies is obvious in their nature, but in a situation where you have multiple offers, and I hope that is the case for you, you will need to pick which contingencies you are willing to accept within an offer.

For example, if you put your home on the market at a price that is already reduced because you know of certain issues that will need to be fixed, and you have a conventional financing contingency that offered $5,000 less than asking price but has **no inspection contingency**, and an offer that is $10,000 more than asking but has an inspection contingency, you will need to weigh whether the issues are going to be worth the potential headache of going through the inspection and the buyer potentially backing out, or just taking the $5,000 less to get the deal done.

Time is another factor with each of these contingencies because each contingency day will push the next contingency back further as well and push your closing date out.

For example if you have a 3 day Condo Rider review period, plus a 14 day inspection window, and a 30 day financing contingency, you're looking at closing at least 45 days out and it could be even further if the lender is backed up with loan applications.

You'll need to decide if you can wait that long, if you'd rather take an offer that's a little lower in price but is practically guaranteed with no contingencies or is an all-cash deal.

If you live in a condo, you will also need to be careful with your **buyer's intended use**. Down here, in Southwest Florida, there are tons of homeowners and buyers who want to rent their condo when they aren't down here, but many associations have minimum rental periods, maximum frequencies, and limited intentional use.

I had a group of buyers who were co-owners of a major electrical company in another state who wanted to buy a vacation home to share between themselves.

We had an all-cash deal with no contingencies and a quick close. While we had an inspection done for their own peace of mind, and applied for the condo association, they were denied approval because for that specific association, they would be considered doing what is legally defined as a timeshare in Florida, and this community voted against their intended use of the property.

Offer-Boosting Strategies

There are some strategies that you can also use to create better offers.

For instance, if everybody who made an offer, offered full price for the house, and all had the same contingencies, you could ask your agent, to counteroffer with a **"Notice of Multiple Offers to Buyers"** form.

This form notifies buyers that the sellers have received multiple offers and would like all buyers to submit their best and final offers for acceptance. This can pit the buyers against one another to drive the price up, but it can also force some buyers out if they have already offered their best.

Counteroffers

Now, there are many ways to counter an offer—some traditional and some more creative.

The traditional counteroffer is to haggle back and forth with the sale price until you can both agree. This one needs no explanation.

You can also counter with more creative offers, like eliminating certain contingencies, and reducing certain contingency deadlines.

Some examples include asking to reduce the inspection window from 14 days to 7 or asking them to eliminate the appraisal contingency on an all-cash offer.

Another creative counteroffer is to ask them to use another lender who may be able to get them a better rate on a conventional loan with a quicker closing date, rather than having them use an FHA program.

If an inspection contingency becomes a problem for negotiating, you can counteroffer to make repairs or replace certain items in the home or work a credit-back at closing into the deal.

REALTOR Advantage – Lock Your Buyer In

As mentioned earlier in the book, the "Standard" contract is a great tool to lock in your buyer.

The contract provides very little wiggle room for getting out of the contract, but at the same token, it also leaves very little wiggle room for you to get out of as well.

While you've locked in the buyer, you're locked in, and will need to perform certain duties and jump through several hoops just to get out of the contract, including making repairs, getting additional home-inspections.

This is another reason for following our **"Pre-Assurance Program."** When you get to this point in the deal, your buyer is locked in, and you can sit back and relax because you've got nothing to worry about.

If financing is an issue, you could counteroffer with seller financing if it is an option and risk you are willing to take.

This may help certain buyers who did not qualify for more traditional loans programs to take a mortgage out with you, the homeowner, to get the deal closed.

There are other creative ways to counter, but I would encourage you to investigate those on your own or ask an agent about them, as these are beyond the scope of this book.

Accepting an Offer

Accepting an offer is very simple to do.

You, your agent, or the buyer's agent if selling your own home, will present you with the contract, signed by the buyers. They should go over the terms and conditions with you. If you like and agree to the terms, you initial and sign in the appropriate places.

The offer is then sent back to the buyer's agent, and you are ready to move forward with the contingency deadlines and closing process.

Deadlines

Understanding the deadlines is one of the most important parts of the closing process. While you're not out to hurt people, a deal like this has a lot of money riding on it. Sellers can capitalize on these deadlines if they are not met.

Remember that earnest money deposit that the buyer should be submitting within a few days of your acceptance of the offer? That is a deposit that was put on the home so that you would take it off the market. **If the buyers miss a**

deadline, that deposit can be kept, and the house can be put back on the market.

While that is not the best move in most cases, it is a possibility. It can also be a big mistake on the buyer's part if they put a significant deposit down on the house.

For example, if a buyer decided to put down a $50,000 earnest money deposit, and missed their deadline, it might be in your best financial interest to keep the deposit and relist the home. However, I would say that is probably not the most ethical thing to do.

You're in the market to sell your home, and I'm not going to tell you what to do, but you'll need to weigh whether missing the deadline is really worth the financial loss you will be causing the opposite party.

In some cases, it may be reasonable because they have cost you money. In other cases, you might consider offering them an extension to complete their tasks.

Back-Up Offers

Something I generally recommend to clients, especially when financing is concerned, is to allow back-up offers. While the "Pre-Assurance" program will eliminate most contingency issues, financing is unfortunately one that it cannot.

When accepting an offer, you are taking the home off the market. However, buyers know that deals fall through, and in many cases, if they want the home bad enough, are willing to put in a back-up offer.

Back-up offers are great because they provide you with another option, if your first deal falls through. This eliminates having to put the house back on the market and explain to other buyers what happened with the last deal. They can also be a viable option if a buyer is dragging their feet on deadlines and making your seller jump through hoops.

Back-up offers are not guaranteed though, because a buyer at any point prior to acceptance of the offer, can withdraw the offer for any reason.

Overall, they are an excellent tool to ensure the home's sale.

If you've learned one thing...

May I ask a small favor?

I'd like to thank you for reading my book all the way to the end, and there is still one more short chapter left to close the deal like a pro...

But, if you've enjoyed this book and have taken away some actionable ideas and strategies and have a much better handle on selling your home, would you consider letting others know about it?

Here are a few ways you can do so:

You can leave a *Review on Amazon*

Leave a review at *Goodreads*

Share the book's *Amazon link* ***on Social Media***

Or recommend it to anyone you know that might find it helpful!

Reviews on Amazon are extremely helpful, both for readers to decide whether this book will be useful to them, and for indie authors like myself to get the word out and continue creating valuable books for readers like you, so your support and help is greatly appreciated.

Thanks again for taking the time,

Rick Harrison III

Chapter 8 – Closing the Deal

For the most part, I think we covered everything you should and can expect along the process of closing the deal.

There's always a chance that some uncommon or even rare occurrence can come up during the closing process. The only way I would be able to help you in that situation is if I know about it and understand the situation.

If something out of the ordinary does happen, I encourage you to reach out to a local agent, or even me directly, for advice. While I may not be able to answer your question if it pertains to real estate law in another state, I can point you towards someone who will be able to help you in my network.

Completing the steps from the beginning of the book, including the investment in your home with the "Pre-Assurance" package, will put you in a great position to have a smooth selling experience ahead of you.

When it comes time for signatures, especially if you will be mobile and need everything to be done electronically, it may be worth investing in Adobe Acrobat Reader Pro DC, so you can upload pdf files and edit them for electronic signatures.

One last tip I will extend to you is to make sure your communications with agents is in writing via email. Text messages and phone conversations are fine for initial contact, but **make sure you follow-up these conversations with an email so you have a paper trail confirming the**

communications. This can save deals and protect you in many ways.

I also recommend brushing up on the statutes and law for real estate in your state if you plan to sell your own home. It will be a boring read for sure, but it is important you follow the laws and guidelines when marketing real estate and executing contracts.

Next Steps – Moving & Relocation Help

Many of you aren't going to be living on the streets after you sell your home. You may be upgrading, downsizing, or moving to a completely new location.

Whatever the case may be, if you used an agent to sell your home, don't be afraid to ask them for assistance in finding your next home. I would highly encourage you to discuss this early in your listing process, so you aren't stuck renting while you search.

Even if you are looking outside of the state or region, ask your agent if they know of any agents in the area you are looking to move to. Many agents build a large network of colleagues that they can work with in other regions, states, and even countries. With everyone being just 6 degrees away from knowing anyone else in the world, and technology making that even easier, you'd be surprised at how small the real estate world really is.

If your agent doesn't know anyone, a great place to look for both an agent and a neighborhood to move to, is YouTube.

You can start by looking up phrases like "best neighborhoods to live in…" and then add the city or area. Then you can begin narrowing it down to neighborhoods or communities.

Once you've narrowed it down to the neighborhoods you can search for phrases like "ABC neighborhood real estate agent." Many agents nowadays are specializing in certain neighborhoods and have their own niche YouTube channels.

More Information & Contact

If at any point you feel like you need some advice, have questions, or would like to have a professional consultation, I invite you to reach out to me and my team below.

The SWFL Relocation Team

https://www.SWFLRelocationTeamTeam.com

Rick Harrison III, PA
C: (239) 310-5478
E: Rick@SWFLRelocationTeam.com

Dave Bernard, PA
C: (239) 765-5478
E: Dave@SWFLRelocationTeam.com

About the Author

Rick Harrison III is a Licensed Realtor, Published Author, and Podcast Host who shares an incredible passion for serving the community. Born & raised in East Windsor, Connecticut, he presently resides in Fort Myers, Florida. As a pupil, Rick attended the East Windsor High School and is an alumnus of the Southern Connecticut State University with a Bachelor of Science Degree in Education. He has always been actively involved in the niche of real estate and shares a strong connection with the construction industry. Driven by the desire to achieve distinction in every facet of life, Rick drives his greatest inspiration from being able to beat the odds and succeed in the pursuit of excellence.

Rick Harrison embarked on his professional journey from the field of Carpentry and served as a Professional Carpenter for four years. During this time, he was able to attain a substantial knowledge of construction essentials and achieved proficiency in framing houses. Following this, Rick devoted the next four years serving the education sector as the High School English Teacher. Moving back to the construction industry, he went on to become a General Contractor specializing in doors, windows, kitchen, and bathroom remodeling. These experiences and endeavors helped him nurture and develop the skills needed to succeed as a professional realtor,

Rick Harrison presently serves MVP Realty as a part of The SWFL Relocation Team and aims to amalgamate his experience and knowledge to serve clients in exceptional ways. As a real estate agent, he takes immense pride in delivering client-oriented services and leverages his years of industry knowledge and expertise to help home buyers and sellers make the best realty decisions. Rick's primary objective is to assist the clients in achieving financial stability and getting one step closer to owning the home of the dreams.

Rick Harrison is also a Published Author and Podcast Host who is enthused by the idea of sharing his knowledge to help people achieve success, prosperity, and happiness. He firmly believes in the notion of building an equitable community and utilizes a portion of his earning to support underprivileged and less fortunate members of society. As a professional, Rick aspires for furtherance in the niche of Real Estate and aims to own a private Real Estate Brokerage.

Besides this, Rick Harrison is a fitness enthusiast who exercises religiously and aspires to inspire people in shaping their lives for the better. His personal goals include writing an Amazon Best-Selling Book and entering a Physique Competition. Rick is also highly active in the online scene and aims to get his Podcast ranked among the top five podcasts in the real estate industry. Rick is an avid seeker of knowledge who is always on the lookout for an opportunity to give back to the community and spends his leisure time playing golf, reading inspiring books, and learning new skills.

Rick Harrison III is a Licensed Realtor, Published Author, and Podcast Host who shares an incredible passion for serving the community. Born & raised in East Windsor, Connecticut, he presently resides in Fort Myers, Florida and firmly believes in the notion of building an equitable community, utilizing a portion of his earnings to support the underprivileged and less fortunate.

Rick Harrison presently serves MVP Realty as a part of The SWFL Relocation Team and aims to amalgamate his experience and knowledge to serve clients in exceptional ways. As a real estate agent, he takes immense pride in delivering client-oriented services and leverages his years of industry knowledge and expertise to help home buyers and sellers make the best realty decisions. Rick's primary objective is to assist the clients in achieving financial stability and getting one step closer to owning the home of the dreams.

APPENDIX I

Budget Worksheet

BASICS

What Is Your Ideal **Profit**?	$_____
What Did You **Pay** For The House?	$_____
What Is The **Min. Sale Price**? *(add them)*	$_____
Multiply by 1.03 for Closing Costs	
MINIMUM LISTING PRICE =	$_____

ADDITIONAL EXPENSES

Carry Cost *(Mortgage, Utilities, Fees, etc.)*	$_____ X
Number of Months of Average Sale	_____ mos.
Appraisal & Inspection	+ $500
Repairs & Improvements *(Estimates)*	+ $_____
Photography	+ $300
Flat-Fee MLS Listing	+ $500
Marketing Costs (Signs, ads, paper, etc.)	+ $_____
TOTAL ADDITIONAL FEES =	$_____

TOTALS

MINIMUM LISTING PRICE	$_____ +
TOTAL ADDITIONAL FEES	$_____ =
TOTAL EXPENSES	$_____

APPENDIX II

Avatar Worksheet

Use this worksheet to identify the perfect buyers for your home and build a profile that will help you create a pricing and marketing strategy later in the listing process. In each section, write out a paragraph with as much detail about the avatar as possible so you can really begin to identify with him/her/them.

WHAT ARE THE KEY ELEMENTS/BENEFITS YOUR HOME HAS TO OFFER?

Location, Upgrades, Neighborhood, Schools, Features, Curb Appeal, etc.

_____
_____
_____
_____

WHO IS THE IDEAL BUYER FOR THIS HOME AND WHAT IS THEIR LIFE LIFE?

Occupation, Work Schedule, Hobbies, Stressors, Marital Status, Family Members, Renters, etc.

_____
_____
_____
_____

WHAT ARE THEIR PAIN POINTS AND HOW CAN THIS HOME HELP ALLEVIATE IT/THEM?

Multiple Jobs, Single-Parenting, Stressful Work Environment, No Vacation Time, etc.

_____
_____
_____
_____

WHERE DO THEY HANG OUT OR SEARCH FOR HOMES?

Restaurants, Clubs/Organizations, Gyms, Zillow, Craigslist, Facebook Groups, Little League, etc.

_____
_____
_____
_____

WHAT WILL MOTIVATE THEM TO PURCHASE YOUR HOME IN THE NEXT COUPLE WEEKS?

Fear of Missing Out, Market Shifts, Exclusivity, Unique Features, Turnkey, Price Per Sq. Ft., etc.

_____
_____
_____
_____

APPENDIX III

Sample Construction Contract

_____, Homeowner/Officer, desires to contract with _John Smith, ABC Construction LLC_, Contractor, to perform certain work on property located at:

_____

___

1. Job Description

The work to be performed under this agreement consists of the following:

_____
_____
_____
_____
_____
_____

2. Payment Terms

In exchange for the specified work, Homeowner agrees to pay Contractor as follows:

$_____, payable for all labor and materials,

☐   In installments by check as follows:

- Demolition is complete: $_____

- Framing is complete: $_____

- Rough Electrical/Rough Plumbing/Insulation is complete: $_____

- Sheetrock/Painting is complete: $_____

- Remodel is complete:
  $_____

☐ 15% ($_____), Down Payment (materials and supplies)

50% ($_____), Halfway Through Completion determined by:

_____
_____
_____

100% ($_____), Upon Completion

☐ 15% ($_____), Down Payment (materials and supplies) and Paid in Full ($_____) upon Completion

Two days after final inspection, submission of conditional lien release forms from all subcontractors and material suppliers and approval by _____ (homeowner/officer or government inspector).

_____ (homeowner) is responsible for any and all fees and charges ABC Construction LLC or any of its employees or officers incur in attempt to collect payments agreed upon in this contract. Furthermore, said homeowner is responsible for timely payments made within the 30 day grace period after the date of the invoice. Payments received after the termination of the 30 day grace period from the invoice sent date may incur interest or fees.

3. Time of Performance

The work specified in Clause 1 shall be started and completed as follows:

_____
_____

_____
_____
_____
_____
_____

4. Independent Contract Status

It is agreed that Contractor shall perform the specified work as an independent contract. Contractor maintains his or her own independent business and shall perform the work independent of Homeowner's supervision, being responsible only for satisfactory completion of the work.

5. License Status and Number

Contractor shall comply with all state and local licensing and registration requirements for type of work involved (check one box and provide description):

☐ ⊗ Contractor's state license or registration is for the following type of work

and carries the following number:

General Contractor: HIC.0000000

☐ Contractor's local license or registration is for the following type of work and carries the following number:
_____

☐ Contractor is not required to have a license or registration for the specified work, for the following reasons:
_____

6. Liability Waiver

If contractor is injured in the course of performing the specific work, Homeowner shall be exempt from liability for those injuries to the fullest extent allowed by law.

7. Permits and Approvals

(Check the appropriate boxes)

□ Contractor   □ Homeowner

shall be responsible for determining which permits are necessary and for obtaining the permits.

□ Contractor   □ Homeowner

shall pay for all state and local permits necessary for performing the specific work.

□ Contractor   □ Homeowner

shall be responsible for obtaining approval from the local homeowner's association, if required.

8. Liens and Waiver of Liens

To protect Homeowner against liens being filed by Contractor, subcontractors and providers of materials, Contractor agrees that (check one box and provide description, if necessary):

□ Final payment to Contractor under Clause 2 shall be withheld by Homeowner until Contractor presents Homeowner with lien waivers, lien releases, and acknowledgment of full payment from each subcontractor and materials provider.

Contractor shall not:

□ Use a subcontractor without first obtaining a lien waiver or release and delivering a copy to Homeowner; or

□ Use any materials without obtaining an "acknowledge of full payment" from the materials supplier and delivering a copy to Homeowner.

9. Materials

a. All materials shall be new, in compliance with all applicable laws and codes, and shall be covered by a manufacturer's warranty if appropriate, except as follows:

N/A

b. The materials shall consist of the following items:

10. What Constitutes Completion

The work specified in Clause 1 shall be considered completed upon approval by Homeowner, provided that Homeowner's approval shall not be unreasonably withheld. Except for the "retainage amount" of 10% of the contract price, substantial performance of the specified work in a workmanlike manner shall be considered sufficient grounds for Contractor to require final payment by Homeowner, except as provided in Clause 8 (Liens and Waiver of Liens).

11. Limited Warranties

11.1 Contractor Responsibility

Contractor will complete the specified work in a substantial and workmanlike manner according to standard practices prevalent in Contractor's trade. Contractor warrants that the specified work will comply with all applicable building codes and regulations, and the labor and materials provided as part of the specified work will be free from defects for one year from the date of completion.

11.2 Homeowner Responsibility

Owner warrants that all materials supplied by Owner will be of new and standard quality, free of defects and may be installed or applied according to the RESIDENTIAL CONSTRUCTION PERFORMANCE GUIDELINES, (Latest edition) as published by the NAHB and in a time frame consistent with normal installations for these materials.

Owner agrees to have all materials on the job site at least 2 working days prior to installation date by ABC Construction LLC or sub or specialty contractors. ABC Construction LLC will give Owner at least 7 working days' notice of installation date.

All unused materials furnished by Owner shall remain the property of Owner, and all materials delivered to the job address shall be safely stored by Owner.

If Owner fails to have the necessary materials on the job site as outlined above, Owner agrees that ABC Construction LLC may purchase those materials, and Owner will reimburse ABC Construction LLC the cost of the materials plus 15% and travel time to and from the job site to the place of purchase at the rate of $35 per man hour with a minimum rate of $35 and 15 cents per mile for vehicle used to pick up the necessary materials at the next progress payment or final payment, whichever comes first.

Owner understands and agrees to be present or have a representative present when any materials supplied by Owner for use on this job are unpacked by ABC Construction LLC. Owner or representative will inspect those materials for completeness of the order and for damage or for any other defects. If Owner is not present when these materials are unpacked, Owner waives any and all claims against ABC Construction LLC for any damaged or missing materials and will hold ABC Construction LLC harmless against any claims for damaged or missing materials by the Owner or the Owner's representative.

Owner understands and agrees that damage done to any of ABC Construction LLC's or subcontractors' tools or equipment as a result of any foreign object within those materials supplied by the Owner, such as nails, bolts, screws or other metal or very hard objects, regardless of the reason, will be the Owner's responsibility to replace (NOT REPAIR) that damaged tool or piece of equipment. Replacement of the tool or equipment will be within 24 hours of the time of damage.

Owner further understands and agrees that ABC Construction LLC's only guarantee regarding the materials to be supplied by the Owner is they will be installed consistent with the RESIDENTIAL CONSTRUCTION PERFORMANCE GUIDELINES, (Latest edition), as published by the NAHB. No other guarantees of any kind are expressed, implied or included in this contract.

Owner understands and agrees that as the supplier of materials, Owner assumes full responsibility and liability for assuring that the products meet all applicable codes and ordinances.

Any resultant damage to any other part of the structure in contact with or adjacent to the materials supplied by Owner and installed by ABC Construction LLC, because of failure of those materials supplied by the Owner, are the Owner's sole responsibility for repair or replacement. ABC Construction LLC's liability will be for the labor only if it is determined by a neutral third party that the Owner's materials were installed incorrectly by ABC Construction LLC thus causing the damage to the structure.

12. Dispute Resolution

If any dispute arises under the terms of this agreement, the parties agree to select a mutually agreeable neutral third party to help them mediate it. If the mediation is deemed unsuccessful, the parties agree that the dispute shall be settled according to the laws of the state that apply to this agreement.

The reasonable attorney's fees of the prevailing party shall be paid by the other party.

13. Change Order (Mid-Performance Amendments)

The Contractor and Homeowner recognize that:

- Homeowner may desire a mid-job change in the specifications that would add time and cost to the specified work and possibly inconvenience the Contractor; or

- Other provisions of the contract may be difficult to carry out because of unforeseen events, such as a materials shortage or a labor strike.

If these or other events beyond the control of the parties require adjustments to this contract, the parties shall make a good faith attempt to agree on all necessary particulars.

Such agreements shall be put in writing, signed by the parties, and added to this contract. Failure to reach agreement shall be deemed a dispute to be resolved as agreed in Clause 12.

14. Not To Exceed Clause

- The cost of the project as outlined in the scope of work that forms part of this contract shall not exceed the sum of $ _____ plus approved adjustments.

- The price of materials is estimated to be $ _____. Between the date of this contract and the delivery of materials to the project site, if the cost of materials increases by more than _____%, through no fault of the contractor, the price of materials under this agreement shall be equitably adjusted by an amount reasonably necessary to cover any such significant price increases. Such price increases shall be documented through quotes, invoices or receipts.

Where the delivery of materials under this agreement is delayed, through no fault of the contractor, as a result of shortage or unavailability, the contractor shall not be liable for any additional costs or damages associated with such delay(s).

15. Indemnification (Hold Harmless) Clause

Contractor agrees to hold harmless and indemnify Homeowner for all damages, costs and attorney's fees that arise out of harm caused to Contractor, subcontractors and other third parties, known and unknown, by Contractor's performance of the specified work.

16. Site Maintenance

Contractor agrees to be bound by the following conditions when performing the specified work:

Contractor shall perform the specified work between the following hours:

Mon. - Fri.:   7:00 AM – 3:30 PM

Sat: 9:00 AM – 3:30 PM (unless otherwise specified below)

_____

_____

At the end of each day's work, Contractor's equipment shall be stored in the

following location:

_____

_____

At the end of each day's work, Contractor agrees to clean all debris from the work area and leave all appliances and facilities in good working order except as follows:

Contractor agrees that disruptively loud activities shall be performed only at the following times:

Mon. - Fri.:   7:00 AM – 3:30 PM

Sat: 9:00 AM – 3:30 PM (unless otherwise specified below)

 Contractor agrees to confine all work-related activity, materials and products, including dust and debris, to the following areas:

17. Counterparts/Electronic signatures.

This Agreement may be executed in one or more counterparts, each of which shall be deemed an original but all of which shall constitute one and the same instrument. For purposes of this Agreement, use of a facsimile, e-mail, or other electronic medium shall have the same force and effect as an original signature.

18. Seal

Contractor agrees that all agreements between Homeowner and Contractor related to the specified work are incorporated in this contract. Any modification to the contract shall be in writing.

Homeowner: _____ (Seal)

Dated: _____

Contractor: _____ (Seal)

Dated: _____

Notice of Cancellation

Date of Transaction: _____

YOU MAY CANCEL THIS TRANSACTION WITHOUT ANY PENALTY OR OBLIGATION, WITHIN THREE BUSINESS DAYS FROM THE ABOVE DATE.

IF YOU CANCEL, ANY PROPERTY TRADED IN, ANY PAYMENTS MADE BY YOU UNDER THE CONTRACT OR SALE, AND ANY NEGOTIABLE INSTRUMENT EXECUTED BY YOU WILL BE RETURNED WITHIN TEN BUSINESS DAYS FOLLOWING RECEIPT BY THE SELLER OF YOU CONCELLATION NOTICE, AND ANY SECURITY INTEREST OUT OF THE TRANSACTION WILL BE CANCELED.

IF YOU CANCEL, YOU MUST MAKE AVAILABLE TO THE SELLER AT YOUR RESIDENCE, IN SUBSTANTIALLY AS GOOD CONDITION AS WHEN RECEIVED, ANY GOODS DELIVERED TO YOU UNDER THIS CONTRACT OR SALE; OR YOU MAY, IF YOU WISH, COMPLY WITH THE INSTRUCTIONS OF THE SELLER REGARDING THE RETURN SHIPMENT OF THE GOODS AAT THE SELLER'S EXPENSE AND RISK. IF YOU DO MAKE THE GOODS AVAILABLE TO THE SELLER AND THE SELLER DOES NOT PICK THEM UP WITHIN TWENTY DAYS OF THE DATE OF THE CANCELLATION, YOU MAY RETAIN OR DISPOSE OF THE GQODS WITHOUT ANY FURTHER OBLIGATION. IF YOU FAIL TO MAKE THE GOODS AVAILABLE TO THE SELLER, OR IF YOU AGREE TO RETURN THE GOODS TO THE SELLER AND FAIL TO DO SO, THEN YOU REMAIN LIABLE FOR PERFORMANCE OF ALL OBLIGATIONS UNDER THE CONTRACT.

TO CANCEL THIS TRANSACTION, MAIL OR DELIVER A SIGNED AND DATED COPY OF THIS CANCELLATION NOTICE OR ANY OTHER WRITTEN NOTICE, OR SEND A TELEGRAM TO John Smith AT 123 Main Street, Any Town, FL 33333 NOT LATER THAN MIDNIGHT OF _____.

I HEREBY CANCEL THIS TRANSACTION.

_____   _____

Signed   Date

APPENDIX IV

Sample Contractor's Job Description

File Name: John Smith Kitchen

Owner: **John Smith**

Plan Date: **December 21, 2020**

Description: Kitchen Remodel

Estimated by: Richard Harrison

Estimate date: August 14, 2015

1. Resurface kitchen cabinets and corner hutch with lighter stain and polyurethane. Sand down,
Re-condition the oak, stain, and polyurethane. Clean and polish cabinet hardware.
2. Remove old radiator covers and replace with vinyl slip on covers. Replace Electrical Box Wall Plates.
3. Remove paneling and wallpaper to patch, prime and paint. *** CONDITIONAL ESTIMATE: (See Clause 13 & 14 in Contract) If drywall needs to be replaced, the estimated price of labor and materials is subject to increase due to a more complicated repair.
4. Replace 6 Interior Doors, handles, and hinges. Replace door and window casing: sand, condition, stain, and polyurethane. Replace baseboard trim, stain, and polyurethane.
5. Repair wall divider and reducer, sand unfinished hardwood flooring, and seal.
6. Window Refinish: Remove interior casing trim and sill and replace with stained and sealed sill. Refinish window jambs and frames with stain and polyurethane.

Qty	Craft Hours	Unit	Material	Labor	Equipment	Total
1.	Cabinet Refinishing					
Liquid/Sandpaper removal of paint or varnish - Millwork & trim						
84.00	NA@ 12.43	SF	50.40	442.68	0.00	493.08
Brush on natural finish stain on interior paneling, one coat - Stain, brush on - wipe off						
84.00	NA@ 5.292	SF	73.92	225.12	0.00	299.04
Polyurethane on interior cabinets, two coats - Roller and/or brush (200 SF/gal)						
168.00	NA@ 5.712	SF	47.04	241.92	0.00	288.96
2.	Radiator Cover Replacement and Wall Plates - NO Labor Costs					
3.	Paneling Removal and Wallboard Repair, Demolition of paneling - Paneling, Wallpaper, Patch and Repair Drywall					
39.00	LB@ 2.886	SF	22.62	97.50	0.00	120.12
4. Door Installation and Trim - Solid core door slab Installation - Hardware & Trim included						
6.00	2C@ 18.03	Ea	1,224.00	754.20	0.00	1,978.20
Brush on stain on interior doors and windows, one coat - Stain, brush on - wipe off						
60.00	NA@ 2.580	SF	4.80	109.80	0.00	114.60
Latex enamel on interior cabinets, two coats - Roller and/or brush (200 SF/gal)						
120.00	NA@ 4.080	SF	18.00	172.80	0.00	190.80

Qty	Craft Hours	Unit	Material	Labor	Equipment	Total

5. Repair Wall Divider and Floor Reducer
Repair gypsum wallboard - Tape, fill, and finish, Installation

Qty	Craft Hours	Unit	Material	Labor	Equipment	Total
8.00	NA@ 2.920	SF	38.24	124.00	0.00	162.24

6. 2x Window Repair and Refinish
Sealant on millwork and trim for interior doors and windows, one coat - Sand, Condition, Stain, and Brush Seal

Qty	Craft Hours	Unit	Material	Labor	Equipment	Total
14.00	NA@ 2.254	SF	21.56	95.76	0.00	117.32

Project Closeout
Clean-up

Qty	Craft Hours	Unit	Material	Labor	Equipment	Total
1.00	BL@ 4.000	Ea	0.00	83.20	0.00	83.20

Supervision

Qty	Craft Hours	Unit	Material	Labor	Equipment	Total
5.00	--@ .0000	Ea	0.00	207.50	0.00	207.50

Contingency

Qty	Craft Hours	Unit	Material	Labor	Equipment	Total
2.00	--@ 8.566	Ea	0.00	355.60	0.00	355.60

Total Manhours,			Material,	Labor,	Equipment	Total
68.8			1,500.58	2,910.08	0.00	4,410.66

Subtotal:	4,410.66
10.00% Overhead:	441.07
15.00% Profit:	727.76
Estimate Total:	5,579.49
6.35% Tax on Materials:	95.29
Grand Total:	5,674.78

APPENDIX V

Home Inspection Guide

This mini-guide will walk you through the steps to finding a home inspector, building a relationship with them, and taking the steps to ensure your home buying process is smooth and mistake-free.

When Should You Get A Home Inspector?

Whether you are buying a newly built home, or one built in the 1800's, you should always get the home inspected. There are plenty of builders out there who are licensed and insured but do shoddy quality work. Sometimes they sub parts of their work out to other companies, sometimes they are behind in their projects or timelines, sometimes they just make mistakes—whatever the case may be, nobody, and no company is perfect, and unfortunately, quality can suffer.

A good home inspector will protect you from any issue that could cost you money down the road. They are not there to scare you but want you to be aware of what they notice, and what could happen if the issue is not taken care of.

We recommend finding an inspector as soon as you know you are serious about finding a house. Finding the right inspector can take some time, and we encourage you to shop around and interview a few different inspectors.

If you have a REALTOR or real estate agent, reach out to them, and ask them if they have any recommendations. A good REALTOR will have built relationships with multiple inspectors throughout their career.

You want to build these relationships early in the buying process so you can reach out to them prior to getting an inspection done. A good inspector will care about helping the buyers and will generally make themselves available for any of your questions, even if your only touring homes. Many times, they will tell you that you can reach out to them if you have a question while your touring a home or are not sure what you are looking at.

Shop Around for Good Inspectors

We encourage you to shop around for different inspectors. Educate yourself on the different types of licenses and insurances that inspectors carry. Not every license or insurance plan is equal, and there are plenty of ways to get certified and licensed nowadays. Do your due diligence and look up licenses on the state website.

Search the inspector's company, check reviews, and look on the Better Business Bureau to see if there are any complaints or outstanding issues that have not been resolved. Angie's List is still a decent source of contractors and inspectors, so you may want to start there. You can also Google "inspectors near me" and you will get a list of inspectors and their google business pages. Read through their reviews and check out their website.

Once you have found a few inspectors that you would like to pursue and interview, what kinds of questions should you ask them?

Interview Questions

1. How long have they been an inspector in YOUR LOCAL AREA?

Some inspectors may have just moved to your area and may not be familiar with the issues specific to that region. While they may have experience in other states, local knowledge is key and can be the difference between catching a costly issue or not.

2. What certifications do they hold?

There are tons of inspections schools and agencies out there. You want to discover which ones this inspector is affiliated with and what those agencies history and ratings are. Are they locally/nationally recognized? Are they known for producing quality inspectors?

3. What insurance do they have?

Insurance is a big must. You need protection on a purchase as costly as a home. Insurance will not only protect the inspector, but you as the buyer.

4. What kind of reassurance do they offer to back their work and report?

Some home inspection boards offer special programs and guarantees that cover their inspectors. For example, InterNACHI has a "Buy-Back Guarantee" for their inspectors, where if any inspector misses something that costs you time or money, they will buy-back your home. Do some research on these companies and their guarantees.

5. What kind of inspections do they PERSONALLY conduct?

Every inspector is different and may specialize in different types of inspections. Find out what inspections they offer their clients, and then ask them if they recommend any other inspections that they would not personally do.

6. What kind of inspections do they sub-out and why do they sub them out?

Going along with the previous question, find out what inspections they sub out and if there is a good reason for doing so. Some inspectors are extremely good at their specialty and would rather sub out to another specialist to ensure you have the best home inspection data possible.

7. How much are their individual inspections and/or inspection packages?

They say you get what you pay for. Find out if this inspector is the cheapest, the middle of the road, or the most expensive. Then see if they have social proof justifying their price.

8. How easy are they to reach in case of a question?

You are going to want an inspector who makes themselves available for clients. Good inspectors know, especially with first time home buyers, that there is a lot of anxiety, confusion, and questions that come along with buying a home. They will readily make themselves available to you and let you know that it is ok to reach out to them with questions and consult with them on a regular basis.

9. What is their availability or schedule like right now if you needed them to come out for an inspection?

You want an inspector who is busy, meaning they have work and referrals, but not too busy that they can't inspect a home in a reasonable amount of time because every contract has an inspection period that is usually about 7-14 days. If they are booked 3 weeks out, they may not be the best choice for you.

Once you have finished the interview process, choose the inspector who checked off the most boxes and you felt a real connection with. That is your guy or gal!

Most Common Issues to Have Inspected

This is by no means an exhaustive list, but these are the most common issues to have inspected down here in the Southwest Florida region, and items that you should ask your inspector about.

1. Air Quality or Mold Inspection

2. Wind Mitigation

3. Polybutylene Piping

4. Termite and other Wood-Destroying Organisms (WDO)

5. Radon Gas

6. Defective Drywall (a.k.a. Chinese Drywall)

7. Lead Paint (homes built prior to 1978)

8. Seawall and Docks

There are many more inspections you could get, but these are the most common ones and can all save you $10K - $100K+ in repairs.

Before or After the Offer

Something most people do not realize is that you may have the ability to have a house inspected before you even put in an offer on a home. While it is traditional to put an offer in on a home and then have the inspection done, you may have reasons for having an inspection done prior to the offer. Somethings you will want to consider and speak to your REALTOR about if you are thinking of getting the inspection done ahead of time.

1. **Can the homeowner deny this pre-inspection?**

2. **How tight is your timeline and budget for a home?**

3. **Was the home listed "As-Is" or REO**

4. **How will this benefit you?**

It really all depends your situation, but you may also want to speak to your inspector about this as well.

Getting Your Report

Reports may come in many different formats and fashions, but one thing will be consistent if you chose a good inspector—they will all be thorough—maybe even too thorough for you to understand it. The reports should include pictures, specific sections for each room, items inspected, and notes on the condition and efficiency of utilities and appliances.

No matter what format the report comes in, there should be a section within the first few pages that is an overview of the findings for your report. This is where the inspector will highlight the main concerns, if any, and make suggestions or recommendations on recourse or considerations prior to buying the home.

This is where you and your REALTOR should make note of the recommendations for negotiating the contract with the sellers. If certain items are of concern, these may be leveraged to negotiate repairs prior to purchasing or credits back at closing for you to take care of the issues on your own.

Stay in Touch with Your Inspector

Stay in touch with your inspector throughout the buying process. Even if you have already had the inspection done, there are things they can still do for you outside of the inspection itself, like visiting the town/city hall and looking permit records for a property. Certain financing options will not allow a home to be purchased if work was done without permits.

Permits are what proves that work was inspected by a licensed inspector and meets code. If the work were not permitted properly, you could be in violation and late fees or fines in addition to having the work be redone properly.

Talk to your inspector about other things they can help you with and protect you from and what they recommend you get done for the property in question. They will save you tons of money and headaches up front.

ADDITIONAL RESOURCES

Podcast on Home Inspection

Home Buying Guide

Home Buying Webinar

Home Search Website

APPENDIX VI

Choosing An Agent

When it comes to choosing an agent, the most important thing is that you are comfortable with them, and you either have testimonials from people close to you, or you have done your research and have looked into their experience and reputation.

One of the fastest ways to do this is to search "Real Estate Agents Near Me" on Google and look through who has the most reviews and the best rating. But what if you're limited on agents nearby and most of them don't have any reviews on Google? That's where this guide comes in.

Stage 1 – Preliminary Search

- Google Search & Reviews Weighing

- Google Business Page & Posts

- LinkedIn, Facebook, and Website Research

- Author/Book Search and YouTube Search

Stage 2 – Consideration

- Setup A Phone Interview (See Initial Phone-Interview Questions)

- Friend Request on Facebook and LinkedIn

- Register for their Website and Check Their Follow-Up Habits

Stage 3 – Making A Decision

- In Person Listing Presentation (See Listing Presentation Checklist)

- Discuss The Market Trends and Strengths/Weaknesses of the Home

- Review Their Marketing Strategy and Pricing Strategy

- Discuss Commission and Process

- Sleep On It

Stage 4 – Begin the Listing Process

INITIAL PHONE INTERVIEW QUESTIONS

1. **What has your experience been in real estate and selling homes?**

This question will break the ice and is open-ended enough for the agent to expound on their experience more.

2. **What area or home type do you specialize in?**

A good agent should specialize in a niche and area. One who says they sell everywhere generally is the jack of all trades and the master of none.

3. **What sets you apart from other agents in this area and your brokerage?**

This question might throw them off a bit, but they should have at least 2 or 3 things setting them apart that sound unique.

4. **What is the market like right now?**

Any agent that says it's good, or it's tough, doesn't really know. How good the market is, depends on a host of variables (type of home, the location, size, etc.). A good agent will tell you that it depends and will ask follow up questions give you a more precise answer.

5. **What are some unique marketing strategies you've used in the past?**

There should be at least 1 marketing strategy mentioned that you haven't thought of. If you've thought of them all, then they aren't that unique considering this is their job.

6. How comfortable are you with writing complex contracts?

Contracts can get tricky and they are the main line of defense should any legal issues arise during the selling process. You are going to want an agent who is very familiar with contracts and negotiating them.

7. Do you work as an agent full-time?

Your best bet is having an agent who is full time because those agents are fully invested in the sale of your home because it's their livelihood.

8. What other partners would you work with to sell my home?

Good agents partner with professional photographers, appraisers, contractors, inspectors, title companies, and mortgage companies to sell your home. Make sure they have a good network that can not only help you, but help buyers as well.

9. How many clients are you currently representing?

It's good for an agent to have clients, but too many will hinder the attention they can give to marketing your home.

10. Another agent said they could sell my home for $75K more at a smaller commission. Could you to that too?

This questions just asks them to defend their convictions and stand by their own value. A good agent knows their worth and knows a home value should be within a certain range.

LISTING PRESENTATION CHECKLIST

✓ **Listing Interview**

    ○ Basic Info Exchange

    ○ Discussion of the House

✓ **Agent Walkthrough and Analysis**

- o Making Notes of Home's Strengths and Weaknesses

- o Capturing Basic Listing & Contact Information

✓ **Listing Presentation**

- o Comparable (CMA) and Adjustments

- o Asking Homeowners Thoughts On Listing Price

- o Pricing Strategy Based on Data & Research

- o Detailed Overview of Marketing Strategy or Tabled for a More Advanced Plan/Strategy.

✓ **Listing Process Overview**

- o Overview of the Listing Process

- o Discussing Commissions

- o Homeowner Expectations

- o Question and Answer Session

✓ **Sign Listing Agreement** or **Sleep On It**

APPENDIX VII

Pro Open House Guide

Step 1 – Choose An Open House Date

Ideally you will want the open house date to be within the first week of the home hitting the market, but you will want to give yourself at the very least 3 days to prepare. There is some work to be done and some time needed for marketing the open house to reach the most amount of people. Besides choosing a date, you may also consider choosing the time. Sometime evening or night-time showings can highlight a homes features better at night with the right lighting, and can make an excellent cocktail party. This will all depend on your price point and your target audience.

Step 2 - Scout Out The Neighborhood

Take a drive around the neighborhood and locate the main roads and multiple pathways, if more than one, a prospect could take to get to the home. Identify yards and intersections that would be ideal to place open house signs.

Step 3 – Research Local Ordinances

While you want to market the property as soon as possible, you'll need to check with local ordinances to see if you are legally able to place signs in public areas such as medians and street corners. You will also need to find out what the time allowance is on such placements.

Step 4 – Neighborhood Outreach

I'm no fan of door-knocking, but when it comes to hosting an open-house, this is one time where I actually don't mind it. Neighbors tend to be the greatest advocates of your neighborhood so they will naturally brag about your neighborhood to friends, family, and anyone they meet that is looking for a home. Invite them and anyone else they know to stop by for the open house.

Step 5 – Marketing

Whether you are an agent listing a home, or you're the homeowner, you are going to want to market the open house in as many places as possible. If you have access to the MLS through a Flat-Fee MLS or as an agent, that is one of the key areas to market it. Classifieds, like Craigslist and other local news sites, is another great place to market them. You can even post them on Facebook Marketplace, or create Facebook ads for it to reach more and more people. See the Property Marketing Guide for the different ways to create ads.

Step 6 – Prepare For The Open House

Two key materials you will want to have prepared are the Property Brochure to hand out to buyers, and a sign-in sheet. I've created a template for you in the Property Marketing Guide that you can modify and use for your own property. You can also sign up for an account on Canva and browse through the flyer templates they have. The sign in sheet is the most important. This provides you with contact information so you or your agent can follow up with anyone who took the time to come to your open house. You can ask them for feedback on the price, the condition, the location, and any other information that may be valuable in making future decisions to drop the price. Just let them all know you would like them to sign in for the safety of your home and valuables. If you have an agent, let them use you as the reason to have guests sign in. If guests have an agent, the agent may sign in for their customers instead.

Step 7 – Host It And Follow Up

The final step is to host the open house. Depending on your price point, you may consider providing beverages and light snacks for your guests. During the event, offer to answer guests questions about the home and handout the brochures. Be careful not to disclose information that you are uncertain of. If you don't know the answer to a question, you are better off saying you don't know and taking down their information if you haven't already got it on the sign-in sheet. Find out the answer from a professional and get back to them later.

After the guests leave, make sure you follow up with them via email, text, or phone call. I wouldn't wait too long to follow up. Even a full day later may be too long and they may already have another home they've looked at or have in mind. Send them a text first explaining who you are, and ask if they have a few minutes to chat. If they don't answer within an hour, give them a call. Ask them for feedback using the questions below. If they answer, follow up with an email thanking them for their time and feedback. If they don't, send them an email asking them the questions instead.

FEEDBACK QUESTIONS

1. What did you think of the home?

2. How did you feel about the neighborhood?

3. What initially interested you in the property?

4. How did you feel about the asking price?

5. What did you like most about the home?

6. What did you like least about the home?

7. Is this home one that you are considering making an offer on?

8. Do you have any questions I can help answer?

APPENDIX VIII

Top-Rated Local Services

DOWNLOAD MY PERSONAL PARTNERSHIP LIST

I hope you enjoyed the content and materials in this book and found the supplemental worksheets helpful. As I said in the beginning of this book, if there is anything I can help you with along the way to getting your home sold quicker for more money, please don't hesitate to reach out to me and my team at:

The SWFL Relocation Team

https://www.SWFLRelocationTeamTeam.com

Rick Harrison III, PA
C: (239) 310-5478
E: Rick@SWFLRelocationTeam.com

Dave Bernard, PA
C: (239) 765-5478
E: Dave@SWFLRelocationTeam.com

And please leave a review on Amazon, Goodreads, or recommend this book to someone you know who is looking to sell their home in the near future!

www.ingramcontent.com/pod-product-compliance
Lightning Source LLC
Chambersburg PA
CBHW030640220526
45463CB00004B/1587